MANAGING INFORMATION

Managing Information

HUGH GARAI

Illustrations by Andy Gill

Gower Management Workbooks

Published by
Gower Publishing Limited
Gower House
Croft Road
Aldershot
Hampshire GU11 3HR
England

Gower
Old Post Road
Brookfield
Vermont 05036
USA

British Library Cataloguing in Publication Data

Garai, Hugh
  Managing information. – (Gower management workbooks)
  1. Information resources management
  I. Title
  658.4'038

  ISBN 0 566 07740 X

Typeset by Wileman Design and printed in Great Britain by Hartnolls Ltd, Bodmin.

Contents

Preface

This Workbook is the product of a new age, of a new way of working and interacting. Written on trains, planes and in the back of cars, in hotel bedrooms and an assortment of restaurants across the globe, it is a true network book.

My purpose has been to construct a Workbook, within the limits and confines of the paper world, that gives you a framework for self-evaluation and assessment which will ultimately set you free to work in new and more effective ways. The critics of IT often hail the paperless office as something that is moving away from us, proclaiming that the technology has failed and is a menace. Well, I believe that they only have themselves to blame. Working with IT as you would paper is absolutely the wrong approach. A new mindset is required – new modes of operating that go against most of the established wisdoms. The perpetuation of hierarchies, the ring-fencing of information, management by control and a host of paper-related diseases must be discarded. In this new world it is the communicator, the catalyst, the team player and empowering manager who are the champions.

This Workbook is about working smarter and not harder. It is about coping and winning in a world of increasing amounts of volatile data. It is about doing more with less by adopting and adapting new processes and techniques to your circumstances. I have put forward a pattern of examination and thinking, coupled with examples and challenges, which I think will help you create a new management framework. However, like most things that require change, it is all down to you. To succeed means being self-critical, creative, adventurous and being willing to try the new.

But remember, technology is supposed to serve us, and not the other way around. IT is just a tool that should be used appropriately to make us more effective, not enslave or slow us down. It can change your life, your work and your organization – and it should! I hope the guidance contained in this Workbook will help you and your organization to change and become more successful.

Hugh Garai

Introduction

Managing information successfully means getting the right information, in the right form, to the right person at the right time to add value to their role.

This Workbook is about managing information effectively so that you can:

- work smarter, and not just harder and harder
- add as much value and be as effective as possible
- empower your team to work effectively in the information age
- use information technology (IT) as your servant to help you do more – not as your master turning you into a process slave.

The amount of information available and the speed of access is giddying. Although the IT-driven revolution is only just beginning, it is already transforming all aspects of our lives.

While there is no doubt that IT is the key driver of the rapid changes we face, it also offers the means to manage change and stay in control. It is no longer we who have to adapt to compensate for the shortcomings of technology – it is now sophisticated enough to be bent, or bend, to our needs.

Not only is IT relentlessly forcing the pace of change, it is also expanding the number of potential futures. As a result, we are travelling increasingly fast towards less and less predictable futures. While we may enjoy the sensation of fear as we are hurled round on a theme park terror ride, in our day-to-day lives we prefer stability to massive and unpredictable change.

So you can either view this new world as a threat ('How can I cope?') or as an opportunity ('What's in it for me?'). Moreover, you can ask, 'What does it mean for my family, my company, its customers and the people I interact and work with?' In other words, 'How will it change my life and world?'

If you see the IT revolution as a threat and try to run from it,

the tiger will eat you. You can opt out, but you can't escape! If you see it as an opportunity, you will be able to ride the tiger and, by harnessing its strength, keep the initiative.

No one can say the ride will be easy or without danger but the alternative is even worse. This Workbook will help you ride that tiger – IT!

---

*I*nsight: **THE SHIFT FROM MARKETPLACE TO MARKETSPACE**

*Jeffrey Rayport and John Sviokla have described a whole new world of business activity that is being created by IT. To distinguish it from the traditional market***place***, they call it market***space***. In marketspace interaction and exchange are freed from any constraints of location, the need to move physical objects or travel to meet people face-to-face. IT is exploding the opportunities for adding value by changing the three fundamentals of business:* ***content*** *– what companies have to offer,* ***context*** *– how it is offered and* ***infrastructure*** *– the means of conducting the transaction. The manager in the information age must seek new opportunities to add value in these areas through the evolving marketspace.*

For example, Federal Express now enables customers to track the progress of their packages around the world on a continuous basis. To do this costs very little as it merely provides customers with information Fed EX is already using for its own operation. Similarly, credit card companies are able to provide corporate customers with the facility to monitor the use of company credit cards as they are used anywhere in the world in real time. Again, the information is already there; it is a question of finding value-added use for it in the marketspace. Companies like these are rapidly developing their own ***intra****nets to exploit these opportunities. (Harvard Business Review,* **72** *(6), 1994, 141–153 and* **73** *(6), 1995, 75–85)*

CAN WE STAY AHEAD OF THE GAME?

*After quadrupling the size of our brains over some 1.5
million years, we have not significantly increased our brain
size over the last 10 000 years. But technology is in constant
revolution all around us and, as a result, the nature of the
work which we expect our brains to undertake is changing
dramatically. Ten thousand years ago your speed was limited
by your fleetness of foot; today you manage a car hurtling at
70mph along a crowded motorway while tuning the radio,
arguing with your partner and shouting at the children. It's a
lot to cope with. It's a testament to our mental dexterity that
motorway pile-ups are relatively rare.*

THE WORK REVOLUTION

In organizations one of the ways in which this pace of change
is manifested is in almost continuous re-engineering and
restructuring. For example:

- Low flat structures are replacing hierarchies leading to the
  creation of temporary units of diversely skilled people – that
  is, project teams and task forces that come together to create
  the required skill set for a specific task. They last only for
  the duration of a project and then disperse or reorganize to
  tackle another project. Change is continuous.
- Virtual teams and even virtual companies and organizations
  are emerging. Their components may be dispersed globally
  and held together by electronic networking – intranets.
  Geography is constantly reshaped by IT. Again change is
  continuous.

The exponential rate of IT-driven change is reflected directly in
your own job. As a manager you are being asked to do more
and more with fewer and fewer people and reduced resources.
You have three solutions, you can:

- work harder, until you drop – and you will – perhaps
  permanently
  or
- discard, displace or outsource work – possibly missing
  important opportunities – and lose visibility and influence

or

- work smarter by making information and IT work harder for you, making you more efficient and effective and freeing you to do what matters:

  MANAGE – be an agent of change, communicate with people, take decisions, take action, create new market opportunities that were inconceivable without IT.

Insight: **INTERNET TO INTRANET**

Unless you have been unconscious for the last year, you cannot have failed to hear more than you ever wanted to about the Internet. What you may have heard less about is the development of **intranets***. These are the private electronic web networks that companies are developing for their own benefit, and often that of their customers and suppliers, that emulate the concept of the Internet.*

You may survive without the Internet but you will find it very difficult to avoid your organization's intranet. Intranets are significantly reshaping organizations' infrastructure with enormous implications for how we will all work in the future. With the ability to access any information from anywhere such much heralded developments as teleworking may eventually become an acceptable way of working for all members of the organization. And who knows? Even the almost paperless office may be viable!

An example of an intranet is BBC's Gateway. Increasingly, BBC staff will be able to use Gateway through the use of browsers, like those of the Internet, to access: the weekly newspaper; a jobs database from which they can apply for vacancies direct via the intranet to the department concerned; a training database that will be able to provide on-demand training and online versions of personnel handbooks which staff will soon be able to question on issues that concern them and receive personalized responses via the intranet. (People Management, *30 May 1996*)

Throughout this Workbook you will see examples of electronic networking or intranets profoundly affecting the way we work.

---

*I*nsight: **IT IS CHANGING EVERYTHING**

Smartcards herald the end of the bank

Smartcards, already widely used in France and Japan and being trialled in the UK as Mondex cards, make the work of the traditional bank clerk obsolete. Such cards automatically manage the transactions through your bank account. They're your bank account in your wallet. So what's a bank for? What new opportunities are banks exploiting in marketspace?

Getting round your doctor's receptionist

Similar smartcards are capable of holding your entire medical history including X-ray and scan images. Why have all the inconvenience and trauma of getting past your doctor's receptionist when you could consult your doctor online? No more 'I'm sorry we can't find your records'. In the US remote surgeries can link patients to specialists thousands of miles away and conduct a detailed consultation with the aid of video conferencing. Healthcare provision is set to be revolutionized by IT.

Typing pool

Has anyone seen one recently?

The personal secretary

Did you once have one?

THE MIDDLE MANAGER IS DEAD! LONG LIVE THE MIDDLE MANAGER?

Machines, once limited to replacing manual labour on the factory floor, are now smart enough to replace the mental labour of middle managers. In the current round of downsizing, middle management represented 20 per cent of the lay-offs although only making up 10 per cent of the workforce.

With electronic networking the most junior people in the company can directly access anyone they wish, bypassing middle managers. Once regarded as the gatekeepers of the organization, middle managers are now seen as an impediment to change. IT sidelines their function, value and prestige. For example, those traditional pillars of society, bank managers, are now becoming obsolete because expert lending appraisal systems, able to draw on the full sum of their bank's lending skills, instantly do a better job faster. To survive, middle managers will have to find new ways to exploit information and add value in innovative ways.

WHAT THIS WORKBOOK WILL ENABLE YOU TO DO

This Workbook will enable you to harness the power of information technology to manage effectively in a world of rapid and unpredictable change and equip you with the knowledge and insights to be a better and more effective manager.

Part I shows you how to identify the information you need to perform effectively.

Part II helps you develop ways of using IT to stay in control and enhance your competitiveness.

Part III shows you how to spread the use of IT through your team and organization to enable them to work more effectively.

Specifically, once you have completed this Workbook, you will be able to:

- identify the information you need for your role
- develop the most effective way to obtain, organize and use that information
- make IT work for you to help you work smarter, not harder
- improve your competitive position and responsiveness
- design your own systems for managing information to suit your needs and those with whom you work
- help others to manage information effectively
- gain some insights into future possibilities in terms of future technologies and their impact on you and the way you work with people.

HOW TO USE THIS WORKBOOK

This book is designed to adapt to your needs, regardless of your position or experience.

If you want to gain new information and ideas quickly or to check up on your own knowledge, you can take the **Fast Track** route. This will take about 90 minutes. As you may well not have 90 minutes to spare at one time, the Workbook is divided into self-contained units which can each be completed in about 10 minutes, perhaps during a coffee break.

Alternatively, if you want to spend more time consolidating some particular skills or implementing certain action plans, you can take the **Skillbuilder** route. This will involve you in a range of activities designed to help you develop ways of managing information and harnessing information technology for your own benefit. You may wish to spend several weeks taking this route, actively developing your systems and techniques to achieve your goal.

You can, of course, switch between Fast Track and Skillbuilder as appropriate.

Skillscan, on pages 10 – 11, enables you to assess which parts of the book are most relevant to you and helps you plan your learning.

Maintaining your skill, on page 207, allows you to review what you have achieved on completing the Workbook and suggests ways of maintaining your momentum for the future.

Extending your knowledge, on page 211, provides a bibliography of useful further reading.

CHANGESCAN: HOW SLIPPERY IS YOUR SLOPE?

For an idea of the pace and scale of change affecting you, consider, by completing the table below, what changes have taken place and affected you in the last 12 months and what changes you anticipate in the next 12 months. Then see if you can construct a similar view of the past 10 years.

Changes over the last 12 months					
Change	Cause	Personal impact	Significance of impact (high/med/low)	Action taken in response to change	Level of stress (high/med/low)

Anticipated changes in the next 12 months					
Change	Cause	Personal impact	Significance of impact (high/med/low)	Action to take in response to change	Level of stress (high/med/low)

Don't worry if your responses show that you are experiencing a maelstrom of change; using this Workbook will help!

SKILLSCAN

Use the following brief questionnaire to assess your level of skill in managing information, to identify which units of this Workbook will be most relevant to you and to set priorities for your learning.

Assess your skill level by circling the appropriate number for each skill area.

Skill area	Skill level					Unit	Priority	Date to complete
	High				*Low*			
Identifying the difference between useful information and distracting or irrelevant data	1	2	3	4	5	1		
Applying the four principles of information management	1	2	3	4	5	1		
Accessing, refining and processing information to achieve goals	1	2	3	4	5	2		
Discarding, transmitting and communicating information effectively	1	2	3	4	5	3		
Auditing the value of information required to do a job or task	1	2	3	4	5	4		
Managing the in- and outflow of information needed to perform effectively	1	2	3	4	5	5		
Minimizing paperwork and organizing information flow and retrieval	1	2	3	4	5	5		
Coordinating activities in a decentralizing organization	1	2	3	4	5	6		
Using information technology to enhance competitiveness by creating more time for people and reducing travelling time	1	2	3	4	5	6		

Skill area	Skill level					Unit	Priority	Date to complete
	High				*Low*			
Harnessing information technology to manage inventiveness and creativity	1	2	3	4	5	7		
Managing and developing people effectively at a distance with the aid of IT	1	2	3	4	5	8		
Implementing a coherent plan to manage information and to become a manager in the information age	1	2	3	4	5	9		

Becoming an Information Manager

Part I will show you how to:

- distinguish between data and information
- understand the four principles of information management
- apply the six methods of handling information effectively
- identify what information you need to do your job
- find, retrieve, sort and format the information you require.

Introduction

*'uniheap' – requiring only attention to category and classifi-
cation – plus a good search and sort algorithm. A uniheap
requires no space, no bureaucracy and virtually no cost.*

*I*nsight: **CONTACTS, CONTACTS . . . EVERYWHERE**

*We can now meet (electronically) more people in a day than
we would have expected to see in a month only 50 years ago.
We communicate more, organize more and travel more than
ever before. The number of contacts and possibility for
further communication increases as the square of the total:*

$$C = N(N-1)/2 \sim N^2/2$$
where C = no. of potential interactions
      N = no. of contacts.

*So with 10 contacts there are 45 possible interactions
between individuals, with 100 it is 4950 and so on. How
many people do you communicate with or know? What are
the implications for the way you organize your work?*

In this unit you will:

- **gain an understanding of what information is**
- **learn to distinguish information from data**
- **consider the four principles of information management and see how they apply in your own job.**

What is Information?

Information is a resource and as such it is not, it becomes. What does this mean? It means information only becomes a resource when it's of value to you. It ceases to be a resource as soon as you don't need it.

Managing Information

The skills you need to work smarter are:

- to distinguish between useful information and data
- to sort, order and display information in the most communicative way
- to identify innovative ways of using information to add value.

All information starts as data. To be useful and powerful data has to be converted into information, knowledge, understanding, communication and intelligence. This is the essence of managing information.

You cannot be swamped by information, only by data. Data that is not yet relevant is raw material to be left where it is or stored away until needed. Information that is no longer relevant is waste data that should be disposed of.

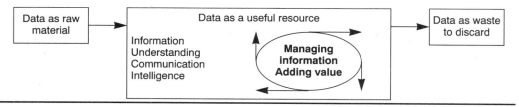

*I*nsight: **THEY COME . . .**

Oil is one of our most treasured resources. But it was more of a nuisance than anything else until a use was found for it – only then did it become 'black gold'.

And they go . . .
Copper has long been a valued resource in the telecommunications industry as the conducting medium in cables and open lines. Its value is now disappearing as optical fibres take its place.

If the value of physical resources is transitory, how much more so is the value of intangibles such as information. Information is both highly volatile and transitory – and so is its value.

'Moses led the children of Israel into the desert for forty years, until they reached the promised land. He had brought them to the only place in the Middle East without oil under it. What a visionary!' (Golda Meir, former Prime Minister of Israel)

---

*I*nsight: **HAVING YOUR CAKE AND EATING IT**

Although the value of information is volatile, it has one tremendous advantage over physical resources – it is not diminished by use. Oil can be turned into thousands of products through the process of distillation but, after each stage, there is less raw material for the next. Information is different – you can use it as often and in as many ways as you like and nothing is lost.

This potential to have your cake and eat it gives managers limitless opportunities to add value in marketspace. Managers who do not seize these opportunities are likely to lose both!

The Four Principles of Information Management

There are four principles of information management. By applying these principles you can turn worthless data into powerful intelligence which, when applied, will generate effective change.

PRINCIPLE 1

Data becomes information by means of the following process:

Data + Relevance + Purpose = Information

- Unless the data in front of you relates to your current need, it is not information.
- Unless the data in front of you can be usefully applied to your current need, it is not information.

This is illustrated in the simple example below:

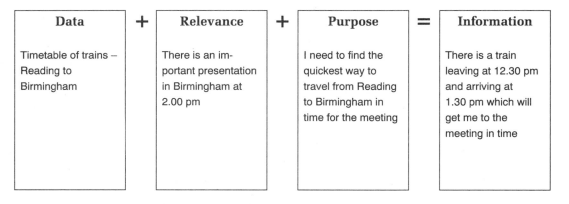

Data	+	Relevance	+	Purpose	=	Information
Timetable of trains – Reading to Birmingham		There is an important presentation in Birmingham at 2.00 pm		I need to find the quickest way to travel from Reading to Birmingham in time for the meeting		There is a train leaving at 12.30 pm and arriving at 1.30 pm which will get me to the meeting in time

Information, once it comes into being, is made increasingly powerful by the application of the following three principles.

PRINCIPLE 2

Information + Insight = Understanding

Information on its own is not powerful. It gains power from your ability to see how the information can be used to develop understanding. This can be seen by continuing the previous example as demonstrated below.

Data	**+**	Relevance	**+**	Purpose	**=**	Information
Timetable of trains – Reading to Birmingham		There is an important presentation in Birmingham at 2.00 pm		I need to find the quickest way to travel from Reading to Birmingham in time for the meeting		There is a train leaving at 12.30 pm and arriving at 1.30 pm which will get me to the meeting in time

Information	**+**	Insight	**=**	Understanding
There is a train leaving at 12.30 pm and arriving at 1.30 pm which will get me to the meeting in time		That means I must leave the office by 12.00 pm before the end of the Task Group meeting		To get value from the Task Group meeting and leave in time I need to reorganize the agenda to make sure that the items most relevant to me are dealt with first

YOU MAY NOW CONTINUE WITH THE NEXT FAST TRACK SECTION ON PAGE 21 OR MOVE TO THE SKILLBUILDER EXERCISE ON PAGE 24

PRINCIPLE 3

Understanding + Communication = Intelligence

Information becomes even more powerful when the understanding it helps generate is communicated and shared with others to whom it is relevant. In this way, understanding becomes intelligence – a superior form of understanding. This can be seen by continuing our example as shown below.

Data	+	Relevance	+	Purpose	=	Information
Timetable of trains – Reading to Birmingham		There is an important presentation in Birmingham at 2.00 pm		I need to find the quickest way to travel from Reading to Birmingham in time for the meeting		There is a train leaving at 12.30 pm and arriving at 1.30 pm which will get me to the meeting in time

Information	+	Insight	=	Understanding
There is a train leaving at 12.30 pm and arriving at 1.30 pm which will get me to the meeting in time		That means I must leave the office by 12.00 pm before the end of the Task Group meeting		To get value from the Task Group meeting and leave in time I need to reorganize the agenda to make sure that the items most relevant to me are dealt with first

Understanding	+	Communication	=	Intelligence
To get value from the Task Group meeting and leave in time I need to reorganize the agenda to make sure that the items most relevant to me are dealt with first		E-mail to Task Group members: to reach Birmingham in time to make the presentation, I must leave by 12.00 pm. I suggest the following changes in the agenda in order to minimize the impact of my early departure		By dealing with those points before I leave I will be in a better position to put my case at the presentation

YOU MAY NOW CONTINUE WITH THE NEXT FAST TRACK SECTION ON PAGE 22 OR MOVE TO THE SKILLBUILDER EXERCISE ON PAGE 25

PRINCIPLE 4

Intelligence + Action = Effectiveness

Information which has been boosted into intelligence and is then acted on has the power to generate effective change. This is the ultimate purpose of information. This can be seen by continuing the example as shown below.

Data		Relevance		Purpose		Information
Timetable of trains – Reading to Birmingham	**+**	There is an important presentation in Birmingham at 2.00 pm	**+**	I need to find the quickest way to travel from Reading to Birmingham in time for the meeting	**=**	There is a train leaving at 12.30 pm and arriving at 1.30 pm which will get me to the meeting in time

Information		Insight		Understanding
There is a train leaving at 12.30 pm and arriving at 1.30 pm which will get me to the meeting in time	**+**	That means I must leave the office by 12.00 pm before the end of the Task Group meeting	**=**	To get value from the Task Group meeting and leave in time I need to reorganize the agenda to make sure that the items most relevant to me are dealt with first

Understanding		Communication		Intelligence
To get value from the Task Group meeting and leave in time I need to reorganize the agenda to make sure that the items most relevant to me are dealt with first	**+**	To reach Birmingham in time to make the presentation, I must leave by 12.00 pm. I suggest the following changes in the agenda in order to minimize the impact of my early departure	**=**	By dealing with those points before I leave I will be in a better position to put my case at the presentation

Intelligence		Action		Effectiveness
By dealing with those points before I leave I will be in a better position to put my case at the presentation	**+**	Attend the Task Group meeting, deal with the important points first, then leave in time to catch the train to Birmingham, well prepared for the presentation	**=**	Arrive in time for the presentation, make an effective case and win the contract

YOU MAY NOW CONTINUE WITH THE NEXT FAST TRACK SECTION ON PAGE 31 OR MOVE TO THE SKILLBUILDER EXERCISE ON PAGE 26

Applying the Four Principles of Information Management: Principle 1

Use the tables below to work out similar examples from your own job.

Data	+	Relevance	+	Purpose	=	Information

Data	+	Relevance	+	Purpose	=	Information

Applying the Four Principles of Information Management: Principle 2

Use the tables below to work out some similar examples from your own job.

Information	+	Insight	=	Understanding

Information	+	Insight	=	Understanding

Applying the Four Principles of Information Management: Principle 3

Use the tables below to work out similar examples from your own job.

Understanding	+	Communication	=	Intelligence

Understanding	+	Communication	=	Intelligence

Applying the Four Principles of Information Management: Principle 4

Use the tables below to work out similar examples from your own job.

Intelligence	+	Action	=	Effectiveness

Intelligence	+	Action	=	Effectiveness

From Data to Doing

Here are the important points to remember:

- Information is a resource and as such it is not, it becomes.
- You cannot be swamped by information, only by data.
- The four principles of information management are:

    1. **Data + Relevance + Purpose = Information**
    2. **Information + Insight = Understanding**
    3. **Understanding + Communication = Intelligence**
    4. **Intelligence + Action = Effectiveness**

ACTION POINTS

Encourage your colleagues to understand the way the four principles apply to their own work by getting them to complete the table overleaf for themselves.

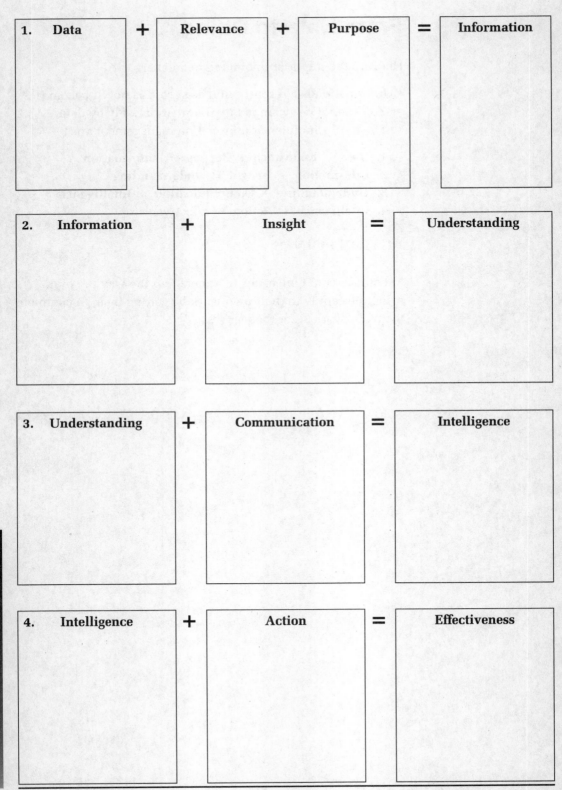

1. **Data** + **Relevance** + **Purpose** = **Information**

2. **Information** + **Insight** = **Understanding**

3. **Understanding** + **Communication** = **Intelligence**

4. **Intelligence** + **Action** = **Effectiveness**

Being an Information Manager: From Prospector to Processor

As you work through this unit you will:

* develop your own databases, responsive to your and your organization's needs
* reduce the volume of data you handle by distinguishing the useful from the useless
* add value to your role by applying information to increase efficiency, effectiveness and empowerment.

The Six Hats of the Information Manager

In managing information effectively you have six hats to wear – namely, those of:

* the prospector
* the refiner
* the processor
* the cleanser
* the transporter
* the communicator.

Unit 2 considers the roles of the prospector, refiner and processor. The next unit deals with the roles of the cleanser, transporter and communicator.

The Prospector

Today's manager must be able to react quickly to events. How quickly and appropriately you can respond will depend on your ability to access relevant information. To do this you need to develop, and know how to access, stores of data. In other words, you need to be an information **prospector**, always searching out the important and valuable.

To do this you should create a database of useful data sources and intercommunicate it with your colleagues and others. However, remember that a database is only useful if it is accurate, up-to-date, relevant and easily accessed. You will have to invest regular amounts of time into maintaining it in good working order – by both adding and discarding data. If you have not used a data source in the last 12 months, you should consider deleting it.

---

*I*nsight: **FROM COAL MINING TO DATA MINING . . . AND BEYOND?**

Whereas 25 years ago the coal miner was seen as the elite worker, today that position has passed to the data miner. Who are the data miners? They are those responsible for gathering, organizing, selecting, synthesizing and distributing information in such a way that it adds value to the organization. However, the outlook for data miners could be as bleak as that for coal miners. Information technology and computer software can do all these jobs much faster and more effectively, producing useful data associations hitherto undreamed of. To survive, data miners must learn to use technology to find a new role for themselves.

Use the following tips when creating your own database:

- **Think ahead.** Try to anticipate your future needs and evolve your database to cater for these.
- Include your past and present colleagues and other individuals who can be an important part of your database.
- You should be part of your colleagues' database too. **Become a valued resource yourself.**

The Refiner

Find out where the useless data is coming from and stop it – for example, remove your name from redundant mailing and circulation lists and Internet newsgroups.

Be ruthless in winnowing out all the rubbish that hits your desk or PC – become a **Refiner**, distinguishing the useful from the useless.

You can categorize all the data you receive according to whether it is:

- **Useless**: If so throw it away immediately – be ruthless.
- **Distracting**: If it's not immediately relevant, paying attention to it now will distract you from your current priorities. Don't throw it away – file it for ready access when it does become relevant.
- **Useful**: That is, relevant to a current task. These items are the only ones that you should spend time on.

Seek to improve the timing of distracters so that they arrive when needed. Apply the JIT (Just-in-time) principle to your information flow.

If the right mix of data is not landing on your desk, you should take steps to cut down on the useless and improve the timing of the distracting (this is dealt with in more detail in Unit 3).

With a paper regime, collecting information requires physical space and real estate – these are a waste of money if you are storing useless items. In the electronic world who cares? You can more or less store everything for virtually nothing!

If you are an all-electronic worker, just title data and file it in a uniheap somewhere on your hard disk. At a later time, sort by date and zero access, discard hundreds of never-used items and avoid wasting storage capacity.

YOU MAY NOW CONTINUE WITH THE NEXT FAST TRACK SECTION ON PAGE 33 OR MOVE TO THE SKILLBUILDER EXERCISE ON PAGE 40

The Processor

To add value, the manager of information has to manage the three **E**s of information **processing**:

- Efficiency
- Effectiveness
- Empowerment.

MANAGING FOR EFFICIENCY

The almost limitless amount of data available to you in managing business processes means that their workings are almost completely transparent. With the right application of information, you can scrutinize business processes minutely and adjust them to make them work at maximum efficiency. In this way you add value by getting more and more of the same for less and less.

---

*I*nsight: **INFORMATION FOR PERFORMANCE**

No self-respecting modern car is without a microchip-driven engine management system. Every second, the system collects vast volumes of data about every aspect of engine performance, analyses it and continually adjusts the performance of the engine to ensure the most efficient performance at all times.

The problem is that, eventually, increasing efficiency becomes more and more difficult, requiring ever greater effort for smaller and smaller gains. Furthermore, for a business, efficiency alone is no guarantee of survival. The corporate graveyard is littered with efficient companies which didn't see the future coming. Being efficient means managing the present. To be effective and survive you have to manage the future.

MANAGING FOR EFFECTIVENESS

It is not enough to produce more and more of the same for less and less. As a manager of information, you have a resource with infinite uses. You can produce more and more different opportunities with the same information. The opportunities for added value are potentially limitless; they are bounded only by your ability to recognize what those opportunities are.

Recognizing opportunities and exploiting them effectively yields the greatest long-term gains of all. Not only does this keep organizations alive and vital, but most importantly it improves their prospects of a long life!

---

*I*nsight: **UK LIMITED**

In terms of its output of Nobel prize winners per head of population and volume of significant scientific research, the UK is a very **efficient** *country, yet has failed to thrive as an economy. The reason? The UK is* **ineffective** *at recognizing the opportunities presented and turning them into profit.*

You can search for these opportunities in three crucial areas of your business:

- **Its content** – what business you are in
- **Its context** – how you conduct your business
- **The infrastructure** that supports your business.

Content
The IT revolution is forcing all companies to consider more thoroughly the nature of the business they are in. They often find that they are not in the business they thought they were. To be effective you need to review constantly what business you are really in.

The image shows an insight from Fast Track.

Insight: TRANSPORTS OF DELIGHT

*Transport businesses such as airlines, ferries and railways believe that their business is to get people from A to B. But their **real** business is providing the **experience** of travelling from A to B. Once this is recognized, the nature of the transport business is transformed. This will become increasingly important as IT makes the **necessity** to travel to see or meet people irrelevant because it means that the travelling experience will be the only thing left for the transport businesses to offer. Their success will depend on the quality of that experience.*

Context

The IT revolution has almost certainly already radically altered the way in which you do business, but this is only the beginning. These radical changes in the way you do business may well change the very business you are in.

Insight: CASHBANK TO DATABANK

Traditionally the bank was a place for face-to-face transactions with physical transfers of cash from hand to hand. The development, and almost accidental introduction, of the ATM machine completely altered the context in which personal banking is conducted, and subsequent IT developments have continued this process.

Modern banking does not involve managing personal relationships, however much banks might try (and fail) to convince you otherwise. It's about managing a huge database of information on personal customers and providing customers with electronic gateways into an almost limitless range of services. Success depends on innovative ways of managing the database.

For example, isn't it strange that, for most people, the gas, electricity, water, telephone, mortgage, insurance and pension companies and local council send you demands for payment and then your bank sends you a statement telling you that the bills have all been paid? Your bank is now your personal outsourcing agency, relieving you of the task of handling the payments yourself. Why don't these companies and your bank recognize the opportunities here and act accordingly?

The utilities are beginning to, as mergers move us towards one bill for all services. The banks, traditionally, move much more slowly – they have the potential to become not banks but our personal cash and credit management agencies.

Infrastructure

Traditionally infrastructure has been perceived as meaning roads, railways, water and electricity mains and the like – those essential components that link us and all aspects of the economy together. But IT has created a whole new electronic infrastructure of which organizational intranets are the current manifestation and the information superhighway is perhaps the ultimate vision.

*I*nsight: MAIL ORDER TO MOUSE ORDER

The traditional mail order business relies on the distribution of huge numbers of weighty catalogues by post or courier, ordering by post or telephone and the despatch and return of goods by post or courier.

Such ways of working are ultimately set to disappear as mail order goes indirectly online in the form of multimedia catalogues on CD-Rom or directly online via the Internet. Already there are over 100 shopping 'malls' on the Internet, and there is a potential explosion of such electronic retailing. Buyers can see and hear demonstrations of goods and clothes and order what they want with a click of a mouse. Such developments will force high street retailers, wholesalers and distributors to rethink their businesses. Once it becomes unnecessary to go out to see goods and buy them, what will attract people to go out 'shopping'? To survive, high street retailing will have to provide an attractive experience beyond actual shopping. If, for example, the attraction is a social one, many retailers will need to rethink radically the facilities which they provide.

*I*nsight: MANAGING FOR EFFICIENCY AND EFFECTIVENESS

*In the early 1980s, Lincoln, a large insurance company, had sold 45 000 special ten-year-term policies within a short period of time. In the early 1990s these became due to reach maturity, raising the problem of how Lincoln was to cope with the administrative burden as efficiently as possible with the resources it had available. Using IT, managers were able to plot, in graph form, all the term dates, enabling them to identify peaks and troughs and allocate resources accordingly. The transparency provided by IT allowed the work to be dealt with as **efficiently** as possible.*

*Lincoln, however, went beyond this. It realized that the needs of this group of clients would have changed and fragmented as individuals entered different life stages and styles during those ten years. By investigating its database, the company was able to identify these likely changes and market directly to specific, reclassified groups of clients with new policies designed to fit their current needs. The result? Lincoln retained the business of 35 000 or 78 per cent of its original customers – a very high proportion indeed. Intelligent use of IT enabled the company to manage **effectively** to retain profitable business – the ultimate key to survival.*

YOU MAY NOW CONTINUE WITH THE NEXT FAST TRACK SECTION ON PAGE 38 OR MOVE TO THE SKILLBUILDER EXERCISE ON PAGES 42–44

MANAGING FOR EMPOWERMENT

Are you a boomerang manager? A boomerang manager is someone who is always being struck in the back of the neck by tasks which he or she believed they had finished and dealt with. If this happens to you, you're a boomerang manager.

To be an efficient information manager, a piece of work should only cross your desk once.

In manufacturing much attention is paid to the costs of rework. How guilty, as a manager, are you of rework? What does it cost you in terms of time? How much does it cost your organization?

Cut down on the amount of date you have to sift through by working on the basis of exception reporting. You don't need to interfere when everything is running smoothly – only when something is wrong. Only receive data when processes start to function outside the parameters you have set. This can dramatically cut down on the amount of data hitting your desk.

Always check regularly to make sure that the original purpose for which data is gathered is still relevant. If it isn't, kill the activity. Far too often data continues to be gathered for processes that are no longer operative.

Remember that your role as a manager is to add value to anything you handle. Unless you can do this, there is no point in your paying any attention to it.

YOU MAY NOW CONTINUE WITH THE NEXT FAST TRACK SECTION ON PAGE 51 OR MOVE TO THE SKILLBUILDER EXERCISE ON PAGE 45

Becoming an Effective Prospector

One of the ways to maintain your value is to anticipate the future demands of your role and the potential needs of your organization and to build your own personal database that can respond immediately to these demands.

Use the table below as a template for developing your own personal database. Remember to:

- review and update it monthly
- search for new and valuable associations within the data you have
- cull it ruthlessly for unused data
- share it with others via your network.

Type of data	Location (NB could be someone's head)	Value-added uses	Means of access	Last updated	Last used

The way a database is structured should suit the way in which it will be used. Relational databases have recently been much in vogue because they allow managers to investigate all sorts of linkages between pieces of data. However, maintaining all the linkages carries very high overhead costs. If the prime use of a database is the efficient operation of the routine processes of a business, it should be structured in the way that best facilitates this and at a much lower cost. Organize your own database to help you carry out your most frequent activities better.

The Refiner's Fire

Log everything that passes your desk **and** through your computer (all those e-mail messages) for a day or a week using the categories in the table below.

Item	Useless	Distracting	Useful	If useful, relevance and purpose (added value)

What proportion of what you received was:

Useless:	Distracting:	Useful:

If more than 10 per cent was useless or distracting, note down what actions you can take to maximize the useful and minimize the useless and distracting.

Managing for Efficiency

Use the diagram below to assess how well you use information for efficiency.

HIGH

Sitting on the gold mine

You have done well yourself to reach a high level of efficiency with comparatively little use of information. But do you have an 'It's mine' attitude? Are you a hoarder of information? Do you keep it to yourself? If so, you are crippling your colleagues and the organization.

Add value by using more information in new ways and sharing it with others.

Action to take

Operating efficiently

Well done. You are using information efficiently to make decisions. But you cannot afford to rest on your laurels. You may eventually find that trying to use more and more information to squeeze out more efficiency reaches the point of diminishing returns. You must continue to add value by finding new ways of using the information.

Action to take

Operating efficiency

Working blind

You can greatly improve the efficiency of the way you work by using more information to make your processes transparent.

Action to take

Paralysis by analysis

You have the information but you are not applying it effectively to produce gains in efficiency. You may be suffering from paralysis by analysis. Would you do better with less? You will never have all the information. You have to make decisions based on 70 per cent to 90 per cent at best.

Action to take

LOW

LOW ▬▬▬▬▬▬▬▬▬▬▬ Volume of information ▬▬▬▬▬▬▬➤ HIGH

SKILLBUILDER

Building Effectiveness: Content

Consider the ways in which:

- IT and the development of marketspaces are transforming the content of your business
- you can add value by developing ways to exploit IT and marketspace opportunities to manage the content of your business.

BUSINESS CONTENT	
Now	**Future possibilities**

HOW I CAN ADD VALUE	

Building Effectiveness: Context

Consider the ways in which:

- IT and the development of marketspaces are transforming the context of your business
- you can add value by developing ways to exploit IT and create marketspace opportunities by managing the context of your business.

BUSINESS CONTEXT	
Now	**Future possibilities**
HOW I CAN ADD VALUE	

Building Effectiveness: Infrastructure

Consider the ways in which:

- IT and the development of marketspaces are transforming the infrastructure that supports your business
- you can add value by developing ways to exploit the new infrastructures created by IT and create marketspace opportunities.

INFRASTRUCTURE	
Now	**Future Possibilities**

HOW I CAN ADD VALUE

Straightening out the Boomerang: Managing Empowerment

Mark each item you handle, whether on paper or on screen, with:

- the date and time you worked on it
- the action you took – for example, file, bin, passed to, action taken and so on.

If an item returns to you, check the reasons for this and take steps to make sure that it doesn't happen again. Some of the reasons why an item may come back to you are as follows:

- A colleague doesn't understand what you want doing.
  - Are you communicating clearly enough? If not, take steps to make yourself clearer.
- A colleague passes the item back to you for action or approval because they don't feel they have the authority to act on their own.
  - Have you set clear enough boundaries for action so everyone you work with is clear as to what they can do?
  - Have you sufficiently developed people who work for you so that they feel sufficiently confident to act on their own? If not, take action to coach others to enable them to take on the required responsibility.
- A change in circumstances renders your original work invalid.
  - Did you work on this item at the right time?
  - Can you anticipate changes that are likely to occur and act accordingly?

If you dare, try being even more radical or subversive! For each item that crosses your desk, consider the following:

- Is it worth doing anything at all, or is it just part of an established but useless process? If it is, can you change the system or kill it?
- Is it important, or will it make no difference if you do nothing? If no one has shouted for a response within a week or a specified deadline can it really be important?

Being an Information Manager: From Prospector to Processor

Here are the important points to remember:

- Being able to react quickly and appropriately to events depends on rapid access to relevant information. You can help yourself to do this by being an information **prospector** and maintaining your own database by:
  - reviewing and updating it monthly
  - searching for new and valuable associations within the data you have
  - culling it ruthlessly for unused data
  - sharing it with others via your network.
- Managing information effectively depends on being a **refiner**, categorizing data according to whether it is useless, distracting or useful.
- Managing information successfully means **processing** information to add value in at least one of three ways – increasing efficiency, effectiveness and empowerment.

ACTION POINTS

Use the table overleaf to develop your approach to information management:

MANAGING INFORMATION: ACTION PLAN NO. 1

To become an effective **prospector** I will . . .	
To become an effective **refiner** I will . . .	
To become an effective **processor** I will . . .	

Being an Information Manager: From Cleanser to Communicator

In this unit you will:

- **consider how effective you are at keeping your data mountains under control**
- **work towards matching the ways you communicate to the speed of the technology available**
- **develop ways to make your communications brief but meaningful**
- **consider the impact of digitization on information management.**

The Six Hats of the Information Manager

Remember, in managing information effectively you have six hats to wear – namely, those of:

- the prospector
- the refiner
- the processor
- the cleanser
- the transporter
- the communicator.

Unit 3 considers the roles of the cleanser, transporter and communicator.

The Cleanser

Are you a junk junkie? Your brain has a natural way of getting rid of unwanted information – it forgets. Unfortunately, it is not always a very good discriminator between what is needed and what is not. Consequently, our self-distrust causes us to overcompensate and accumulate information in files and on computers. As a result, our systems become clogged and we spend more and more time searching for – and often failing to find – what is relevant.

Very often the state of an individual's screen (or desk-top) reflects the state of their office, home, car and the way they are organized – or disorganized!

Insight: ARE YOU A SLOB (STORING LOADS OF BUMF)?

At home do you regularly put out your rubbish for collection and disposal or, even better, recycle and compost it, or do you just let it all pile up in your home as a rotting, unhealthy mess? Assuming you don't do the latter, treat the data in your office in the same way as your domestic rubbish – turn it into something useful or dispose of it. That's your role as a manager – to add value!

Consider the value of the information you keep – how quickly does its value decay? At what point do you dump it?

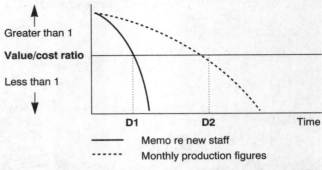

Dump memo at D1 and production figures at D2.

If you find it difficult to decide when to dispose of information, consider this. When you retire how large will your office have to be if you don't dump information?

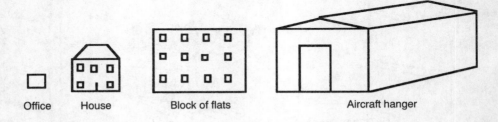

The Transporter

The progression of communication from using footpower through horsepower, train, telegraph, telephone, fax, computer and satellite has meant that the speed at which we can communicate has increased exponentially, but the way we use these modern methods is often out-of-date. What we actually do does not match what we **can** do.

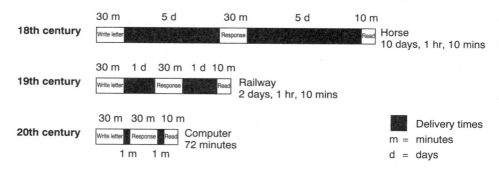

In the past it was delivery time that dictated the speed of communication. That is no longer the case – nowadays delivery can be virtually instantaneous and it is now our ability to process work that's the limiting factor. Improvements here depend on working smarter, not harder – so any further improvement in speed is down to you!

Insight: **FROM 12 DAYS TO 12 HOURS**

Then . . .
In the civil service the prime means of communication was paper, usually in triplicate, with the time needed to move letters and notes between departments typically 12 days or more. Why 12 days? Because even for a senior manager having the letter dictated, typed, corrected and signed off would take three days. For junior managers, having to use the typing pool, this would typically extend to five days. The internal and external mail system would then take a further two days or more for delivery. If the letter was started on a Monday, it would not be posted until Friday. It would then arrive the following Monday, for the whole process to start again.

Now . . .
'My average response time to any communication is about three and a half hours. I have replaced over 80 per cent of my external communication with electronic mail, 99 per cent of which – both internal and external – I complete within 12 hours.' (Peter Cochrane)

The Communicator

Taking ideas, concepts and information and communicating clearly to others is a complex and difficult undertaking. Most people can be convinced more quickly by pictures rather than words, but if you have to use words, make them short and keep the message succinct.

Is your communication style appropriate to the technology you use and the speed at which you need to communicate? There is little point in being able to send an instantaneous message if it takes hours to understand at the other end.

Use as few words as possible – make use of bullet points, large print, pictures, graphs – in other words, make it easy.

*I*nsight: **HIT THE HEADLINES!**

The Brazilian entrepreneur Ricardo Semler encourages all his managers to use short and attention-grabbing newspaper-style headlines when writing memos – for example, **£20 000 investment saves 3 days on each project.** *Need one say more?*

When writing a communication ask yourself: 'How would I like to receive this? Would I understand it? Would I begrudge the time taken to read it?' **Remember P1000 – a picture is worth a 1000 words – and, better still, AP1 000 000 – an animated picture is worth a 1 000 000 words.**

Constantly review what you want to communicate to make sure it is brief and to the point. People scan rather than read, so you need to catch their eye. Always **KISS** (**K**eep **I**t **S**imple, **S**tupid) those with whom you communicate. You will save yourself and others a great deal of time.

In experiments with letters, newsprint and other forms of documentation, a computer précis process showed that 98 per cent of the information was retained by using just 24 per cent of the words. The following example shows how information can be compressed without losing meaning.

Letter	Fax	E-mail
Dear Jane I have spoken to Mr Sparrow about the work on the plant. Unfortunately he is unable to attend the meeting on Friday as he will be down at Head Office. We have provisionally pencilled in the week of 8 January as the most appropriate time to start work. Following that I would expect the foundations to be in place by mid-February. I attach an amended schedule. As you will see, we have been able to reduce the costs considerably on the basis of the amended plans. If this schedule meets with your agreement, I will contact Mr Sparrow and provide him with details of the plans so that he can brief the relevant staff. Yours sincerely *(119 words) (100%)*	Jane Spoken to Sparrow re work on plant. Sparrow unable to attend meeting on Friday as he is at HQ. Plan to start work w/b 8 Jan. New schedule attached – note reduced costs. If you agree I'll give Sparrow plans so he can brief his staff. *(46 words) (39%)*	Told Sparrow re plant works S ≠ Friday meeting S = HQ Friday Plan = start w/b 8 Jan. New schedule attached = reduced costs. If you agree, S gets plans to brief staff. *(34 words) (28.5%)*

Remember – if you don't communicate well, you will have to explain again, thereby wasting even more time, and you may propagate errors, misunderstanding and confusion. You may even do some damage to yourself, your customer and your organization. Often 10 per cent more effort upfront can save you in excess of 50 per cent at the back end of this process. IT now gives you the means to present most data visually, making assimilation and understanding much quicker and easier.

YOU MAY NOW CONTINUE WITH THE NEXT FAST TRACK SECTION ON PAGE 56
OR MOVE TO THE SKILLBUILDER EXERCISE ON PAGES 61–62

Managing in a Digitized World

Managing information in the age of IT requires a totally different mindset and a willingness to use the new tools to create new working methods and regimes. The IT world is about constant change and experimentation, and opening up new potentials and possibilities.

The manager of information in the digitized world needs all of the six hats described in these last two units.

---

*I*nsight: **MANAGING IN A DIGITIZED WORLD**

Xerox has been repositioning itself as 'The Document Company' in recognition of the fact that, according to Peter Van Cuylanburg, digitizing technology has led to a fundamental shift in the way we need to view documentation. It also means that printing and production can be decentralized towards the customer. Why buy a book when you only need a chapter? Why buy a journal when you only want to read an article?

Digitized information is networked information, capable of simultaneous infinite manipulation to meet the needs of potentially countless end-users who may interact with the data together or separately. The digitized document becomes **the** *interface between people and the processes they manage, accessed via the organization's intranet. (Financial Times, 1 November 1995)*

The digitized document goes through three phases, each defined by particular technologies as shown in the diagram below:

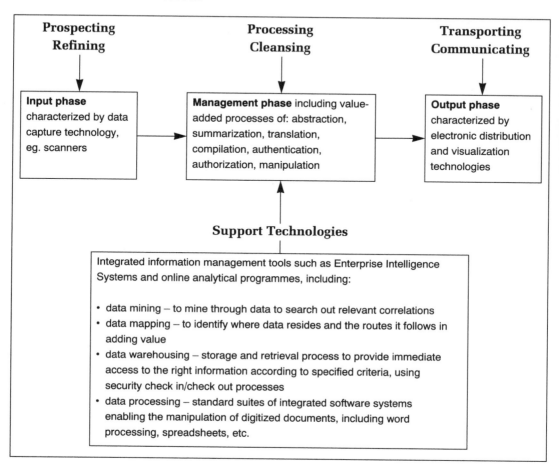

Prospecting Refining

Input phase characterized by data capture technology, eg. scanners

Processing Cleansing

Management phase including value-added processes of: abstraction, summarization, translation, compilation, authentication, authorization, manipulation

Transporting Communicating

Output phase characterized by electronic distribution and visualization technologies

Support Technologies

Integrated information management tools such as Enterprise Intelligence Systems and online analytical programmes, including:

• data mining – to mine through data to search out relevant correlations
• data mapping – to identify where data resides and the routes it follows in adding value
• data warehousing – storage and retrieval process to provide immediate access to the right information according to specified criteria, using security check in/check out processes
• data processing – standard suites of integrated software systems enabling the manipulation of digitized documents, including word processing, spreadsheets, etc.

YOU MAY NOW CONTINUE WITH THE NEXT FAST TRACK SECTION ON PAGE 69 OR MOVE TO THE SKILLBUILDER EXERCISE ON PAGE 63

Cleaning out the Stables

You must develop the habit of regularly dumping information from all your files whether in cabinets or computers. Remember, the more waste data there is on your computer system the slower it will perform and the less able it will be to respond to you.

Start by looking at the thickness of paper files and Mbytes of computer files and try halving them – just throw out what you don't need. Sort by date – if you haven't accessed or used an item in three or six months, why are you keeping it? It's probably out-of-date and dangerous. Look out for duplication and multiple versions and copies – the most dangerous form of information pollution!

Adopt a TFR – a Tidy Friday Routine. And remember, **Friday may be any day or every day!**

It's not enough for you to do it on your own, make sure everyone else does too.

PLOT YOUR PROGRESS

Today (or as soon as you can):

- Pile all your files and other papers into one stack and measure and record the height.
- Add up the Mbytes of memory used by all your computer files and note down the total.
- Construct a graph, as in the example below, and put the total height of your paper stack and Mbytes used at the top of each of the vertical axes. Draw a line horizontally across representing 50 per cent of the total. That's your immediate target – to halve the size of your files.
- Get all your colleagues to do the same and set up a competition to see who can reduce their files the most. Give a prize to the winner.

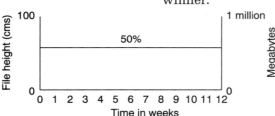

When you've achieved this target, try to reduce by another 50 per cent! See how far you can get. Plot your progress on your graph each week and display it somewhere prominently.

> If you want to be really radical, remove 50 per cent of the photocopiers and printers. Then remove half of the filing cabinets. Then reduce the floor space per person by 20 per cent. Finally, move to smaller premises, where you'll probably find that you can give everyone 10 per cent more space than they had before!

> Don't make others do unnecessary work. If you no longer need a specific report or set of data, tell the originator so that he or she can save time and do something useful instead.

The Transporter: Turnaround

Use the flow diagram below to work out the normal response time for your internal and external communications. Use the space on the right to construct a flow diagram for a response system that will halve your current response time.

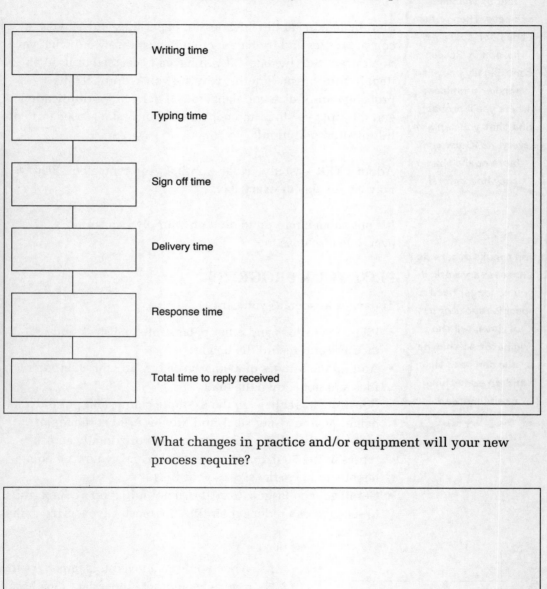

Writing time

Typing time

Sign off time

Delivery time

Response time

Total time to reply received

What changes in practice and/or equipment will your new process require?

The Communicator: Keep It Brief

Use the template below to:

- write a business letter of not more than 250 words
- make a fax of your letter of no more than 125 words or 50 per cent of the letter
- make an e-mail of your letter of no more than 60 words or about 25 per cent of the letter.

Show your efforts to your colleagues to check that the important information has not been lost in the compression.

The more you practise conciseness and demand it from others, the less time you will have to spend on formal communication.

Letter	Fax	E-mail

Now, look at other people's reports and presentations to see how many words you can remove and what pictures could have been used to help you understand more quickly. Record the time from the first word to the point where you first understand the whole communication. You could also do this with your colleagues as a team or departmental exercise to improve communication.

Report/presentation	No. of words	Time taken to understand

Note: There is a developing etiquette involved in using e-mail and the Internet. Take care not to offend others. Find out what are the acceptable conventions and remember that e-mail messages can sound very terse and impersonal, especially to those you don't know. With people you do not know well, it is safer to edge towards a concise and businesslike style rather than leap in straightaway.

Managing in a Digitized World

Use the diagram below to assess to what extent you are, or should be, using the data manipulation technologies available to add value to your information management.

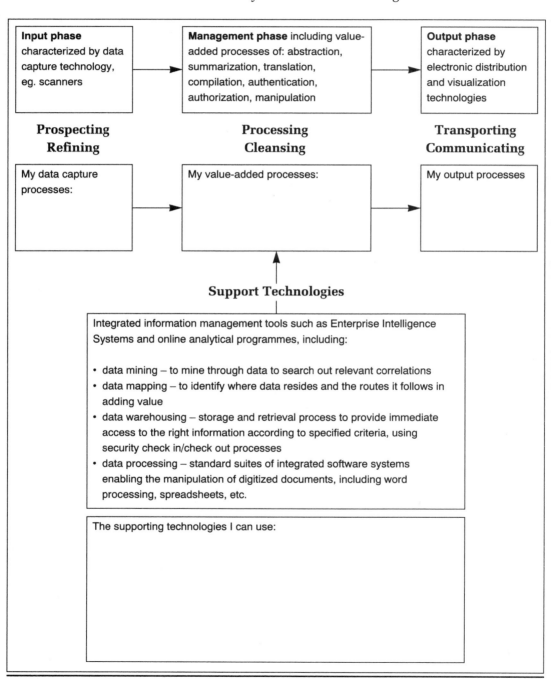

| **Input phase** characterized by data capture technology, eg. scanners | **Management phase** including value-added processes of: abstraction, summarization, translation, compilation, authentication, authorization, manipulation | **Output phase** characterized by electronic distribution and visualization technologies |

Prospecting Refining   **Processing Cleansing**   **Transporting Communicating**

My data capture processes:

My value-added processes:

My output processes

Support Technologies

Integrated information management tools such as Enterprise Intelligence Systems and online analytical programmes, including:

- data mining – to mine through data to search out relevant correlations
- data mapping – to identify where data resides and the routes it follows in adding value
- data warehousing – storage and retrieval process to provide immediate access to the right information according to specified criteria, using security check in/check out processes
- data processing – standard suites of integrated software systems enabling the manipulation of digitized documents, including word processing, spreadsheets, etc.

The supporting technologies I can use:

Being an Information Manager: From Cleanser to Communicator

Here are the important points to remember:

- You need to take control of the data you accumulate and **cleanse** it on a regular basis from your paper and PC files.
- Over the last 200 years the speed at which we can transmit information has increased exponentially. To take advantage of this, you have to become a modern **transporter** of information, matching your communication processes to the new technology.
- The key to good communication is quick understanding. Develop ways to **communicate** information that make it as quick and easy as possible to understand – use modern technology to convert words into pictures, graphs and animations.

ACTION POINTS

Use the table overleaf to develop your approach to information management:

MANAGING INFORMATION: ACTION PLAN NO. 2	
To become an effective **cleanser** I will . . .	
To become an effective **transporter** I will . . .	
To become an effective **communicator** I will . . .	

In this unit you will:

- identify the information you need to do your job
- use a seven-step framework to assess the information in terms of its purpose, accessibility and mode of communication.

Introduction

To work smarter you have to control the information you need. To do this you must answer the following questions:

- What information do I need?
- Why do I need it?
- How will I use it?
- From whom/where can I get it?
- When do I need it?
- In what form do I need it?
- What information do others need from me? (This includes asking 'Why?, When? and How?)
- What unnecessary data am I receiving?
- What useful and necessary information am I getting too slowly, in the wrong form and so on?
- Who should I communicate it to, in what format and by what means?
- What filters can I put in place to deflect or divert information?

To conduct a successful audit you can use the following seven-step framework to analyse exactly what information you need in your job or to complete a task, and how you will use that information effectively.

The framework is divided into four areas:

- The **Purpose** of the information   P
- How it can be **Accessed**   A
- How added value can be **Communicated** to others   C
- **Evaluating** results for continuous improvement   E

At the end of this unit 'Action Points' (page 88) gives a blank framework which you can use to conduct your own audit.

Step 1: Purpose – 1

WHY DO I NEED IT?

The process of gathering information can be used as a useful management tool enabling your team to recognize the information that is important to you and its significance.

You must be sure of why you need a particular piece of information. We all tend to accept huge amounts of purposeless data which clog up our work and often prevent us from receiving information that we really do need. An effective manager is one who can select information efficiently and add value by applying it effectively.

Don't be a 'just-in-case' case
Resist the temptation to hoard information on the basis that, although you don't know what to use it for now, it might come in useful later. The chances are that 'later' – like tomorrow – will never come and, if it does, the information will probably be out-of-date by then.

If you really are a squirrel and cannot live without hoarding absolutely everything, then buy a scanner and a CD burner. Create yearly CDs containing everything you did. Low-cost CDs have a capacity of 630 Mbytes – about half the contents of an encyclopaedia. The next generation will be 7000 Mbytes – try filling that!

1. Why do I need it?
To prevent yourself being overwhelmed you must be ruthless in assessing the value of each piece of data. Unless it directly contributes to achieving a specific objective, reject it.

Key question:
Can I achieve my objective without this data?
If your answer is 'yes' – reject it.

How many people in your office or organization have hard copies of exactly the same material? Why have multiple copies of anything within walking distance? Real estate costs a lot of money!

YOU MAY NOW CONTINUE WITH THE NEXT FAST TRACK SECTION ON PAGE 70 OR MOVE TO THE SKILLBUILDER EXERCISE ON PAGE 79

Step 2: Purpose – 2

HOW WILL I USE IT?

Information is a tool – use it like one, but remember that all tools are designed with a specific purpose in mind.

Are you using the right tool for the job? (*Is a sledgehammer appropriate for knocking in panel pins?*) How much information do you need to make a simple decision? It is not unusual for someone to spend £1 000 making a decision to spend £100!

Is the tool in good enough repair to do the job? (*It's difficult to cut straight with a blunt saw.*) If your information is out-of-date, so is your decision.

Should the tool be used in conjunction with others? If so, what are they and do you have them? (*You often need a spanner and a screwdriver to tighten up nuts and bolts. Knowing it's going to rain, you might take an umbrella. Knowing it's going to rain and blow a force 10 gale, you might stay at home!*)

*I*nsight: DATAWEAR

At Jaeger, the fashion clothes retailer, managers have access, through a series of linked databases, to an enormous mass of data which they can assemble in any way they like. A manager could, for example, find out the number of size 12 short-sleeved pink silk blouses bought by Access cardholders between 2.00 and 3.00 pm on a wet afternoon in April in Bournemouth!

The only value of the data to Jaeger is the way its managers select and use it to add value to the business. Managers add value by assembling the data into combinations that become powerful pieces of information when applied, for example, in the making of particular marketing decisions.

The development of marketspace demands that the successful manager creates new market opportunities from the information available. Perhaps a Jaeger manager will see the opportunity to directly market a new line of pink silk blouses to a certain sector of the population of Bournemouth!

If you think that information can only be used in one way, think again. Think beyond the internal demands of your business to ways in which you could use the same information to open up new market opportunities.

2. How will I use it?

You must know how you will use a piece of information before accepting it.

Key questions:

How will this information help me achieve my objective?
How will it link to other pieces of information?
How will it enhance the value of other information?
How can it be used in entirely new ways to add value?

YOU MAY NOW CONTINUE WITH THE NEXT FAST TRACK SECTION ON PAGE 72 OR MOVE TO THE SKILLBUILDER EXERCISE ON PAGES 80–81

71

Step 3: Accessibility – 1

HOW CAN I GET IT?

Our attempts to make a decision or complete a task are often frustrated because we cannot gain access to the information we need. This could be for a number of reasons:

- We don't know that it exists.
- We don't know where it is.
- We don't have the authority to access it.
- We can't find it in the rubbish heap called our desk, office or filing system!

It is not enough to know what information you need, you have to establish your supply lines and keep them secure.

---

*I*nsight: **CREATING AN INFORMATION WEB**

Production engineers at Jaeger are scattered across a number of manufacturing sites almost from Land's End to John O'Groats. They are dealing with a myriad different fabrics being made into thousands of different styles and types of clothing. Knowing how a fabric is going to behave under a particular production process is crucially important. Although, between them, the engineers have a vast store of information about production issues, accessing it was once a problem . . .

Then . . .
If an engineer at one site wanted to ask another elsewhere about how a particular fabric behaved, he would phone up and encounter the sorts of problem which we all face in these situations. For example:

- *the other person wouldn't be available*
- *if a message was left, it would often fail to get through*
- *if the message was received, as often as not, the person would often be too busy to respond*
- *when the person called back, the original caller would be away from their desk.*

Time . . . time . . . time . . . being wasted.

Now . . .

The solution has been simple and immensely effective.

All the engineers are connected via the company's e-mail system, creating an information web. If a production engineer has found out something useful, by sending one e-mail message this information is passed instantaneously to ALL the other engineers and posted on to their bulletin board.

If an engineer has a query, he or she can either scan the bulletin board and gain immediate access to the full store of knowledge or e-mail to all the other engineers simultaneously and be sure of a quick response from someone. Fruitless, time-wasting telephone calls have been eliminated and been replaced by instant access and quick response.

---

*I*nsight: **WHY DO BEER DRINKERS WEAR NAPPIES?**

Data mining is the process of teasing out valuable information from the mountains of data that organizations can now capture about every aspect of their processes and interaction with customers. Data mining software can find valuable associations between different aspects of the organization that could not be guessed at before. For example, a large American supermarket chain discovered that buyers of a certain brand of beer also had a strong tendency to buy a certain brand of nappies. This was an association that no one could guess at, yet existed. Its identification led to changing the layout of stores to bring the two products closer together, helping to enhance the sales of both. (Financial Times, *4 October 1995)*

---

3. How can I get it?

To achieve an objective you need to secure your access paths to information.

Key questions:
Do I know where this information is?
Do I have the authority to access it?

Step 4: Accessibility – 2

WHEN DO I NEED IT?

Steering a path between distraction and disaster

The timeliness of information is critical. If information arrives too soon it risks becoming:

- a distraction from other activities that are a priority at that time
- out-of-date by the time you need to use it
- lost when you need it.

On the other hand, late information is, at best, no information and, at worst, a potential disaster.

You should plan to receive information at the time when it will be most powerful. You need to take into account:

- how long it will take to assemble
- how long it will take to arrive
- what delays are likely to occur.

---

*I*nsight: **20:20 VISION**

Part of the Allied strategy for the Normandy invasion in 1944 was to keep Hitler's armies guessing about where it was going to take place. Because they did not have the right information in time, Hitler's generals had to decide how to deploy their forces. They made the wrong decision, and the rest is history. If they had obtained the correct information in time and consequently made the right decision, the outcome might have been very different.

---

4. When do I need it?

Information which arrives too early can be a distraction. Information which arrives too late can be a disaster.

Key questions:

How long will it take to get it?
At what stage does it form a crucial input into my objective?

YOU MAY NOW CONTINUE WITH THE NEXT FAST TRACK SECTION ON PAGE 75
OR MOVE TO THE SKILLBUILDER EXERCISE ON PAGE 83

Step 5: Accessibility – 3

IN WHAT FORM DO I NEED IT?

Delays and frustrations often occur because you don't receive information in the right format. The purpose determines the form.

You need to consider compatibility in terms of:

- **The medium**
  - Do you need the information on paper or fed directly to your PC?
  - If it is coming to your PC, is it compatible with the software you are using?
  - If not can it be easily converted or, preferably, sent in the right format in the first place?
- **The measurements** – for example, you need the:
  - measurements in metric and they arrive in imperial.
  - production figures in litres per hour and they arrive in tonnes per day.
- **The precision or detail**
  If your information is too detailed, you waste time trying to grasp the whole picture. If it contains too little detail, you cannot be sure of its content. For example, you might need to know the exact percentage of defects per shift and receive an approximate range figure per day.

5. In what form do I need it?
To be useful, information must come in the right form.

Key questions:
What criteria do I need to set for receiving information?
What compatibility problems may arise?
In what way do I intend to interpret the information?

FAST TRACK

Step 6: Communication

WHO ELSE NEEDS IT?

Unless you are working entirely for yourself, you will need to communicate the decision you have taken, the output from your task, or the information you generate, to others. You are part of a chain and the overall strength of the chain is only as strong as its weakest link.

Unless you are adding value to the process – making the information you pass on more powerful to someone else – you are not managing effectively.

---

*I*nsight: **MAKING A LITTLE GO A LONG WAY**

Jesus Christ was the most effective resource manager ever. He took five loaves and two fishes and fed 5000 men – not even counting the women and children – and there were 12 baskets left over. Now that's adding value!

You should pass information on to others in the same way – getting the most value from the least input. With the help of IT, we can now all aspire to perform such miracles every day!

---

6. Who else needs it?
The outcome of your activities forms the inputs to someone else's activities. To be effective you must be able to communicate with them, adding value to what you pass on.

Key questions:
Who are the links in my activity chain?
How am I adding value to what I pass on to them?
What is the most effective way of communicating with them?

YOU MAY NOW CONTINUE WITH THE NEXT FAST TRACK SECTION ON PAGE 77
OR MOVE TO THE SKILLBUILDER EXERCISE ON PAGE 85

Step 7: Evaluation

HOW CAN I BETTER MEET THE NEEDS OF OTHERS AND MYSELF?

You can think of this question as being the reverse of Step 5 – in what form do I need it?
You need to consider the compatibility of your information in terms of:

The medium
How do your colleagues, customers and suppliers need to receive information from you?

The format
In what format do they need to receive information? For example, are you providing:
– measurements in imperial when they need them in metric?
– the production figures in litres per hour when they need them in tonnes per day?

Precision or detail
If you provide too much detail you waste your colleagues' and customers' time trying to grasp the whole picture. If you give too little detail they cannot be sure of the content.

7. *How can I better meet the needs of others and myself?*
Other people should be completing their own information audit. You need to link up with them to maximize synergy and compatibility and review constantly for improvement.

Key questions:
What can I do to further improve the information that others receive from me?
How can I further improve my own systems?

Step 1: Why Do I Need It?

Choose a particular objective, task or decision that is a focal point of your current work. Use the following chart to help you assess the minimum information you need to:

- achieve your objective
- complete the task
- make the decision.

> **Keep in mind the three categories of information: necessary to know, nice to know and clutter!**

Information I MUST have – **for example:** *I can't make a decision without this information.*	• • •
Information I SHOULD have – **for example:** *I'd be happier making this decision if I had this information.*	• • •
Information I COULD have – **for example:** *It would be nice to know this but, on its own, it won't change my decision.*	• • •

SKILLBUILDER

> **Make sure that the information you rely on is accurate. Always use cross-checking mechanisms to verify its accuracy. Many disastrous decisions can be avoided by cross-checking information on which they are based.**

What if . . .

- you have more information than you actually need or will use?
- you could ignore some information without materially affecting the outcome?

Get rid of it.

What if . . .

- you don't have all the information you **must** have?

Seek alternatives. For example, can the combined impact of '**should** have' and '**could** have' make up for the lack of '**must** have'?

79

Step 2: How Will I Use It? Building a Better Tool Kit

As we learned in Unit 2 (page 33), information can be used in three basic ways:

- to enhance efficiency
- to enhance effectiveness
- to enhance empowerment.

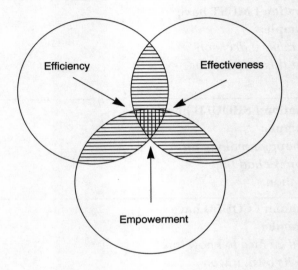

The more ways you can use information the more powerful it is. Consider how you can spread the use of information. Use the diagram opposite to work out how to obtain the maximum added value from all the information you use.

SKILLBUILDER

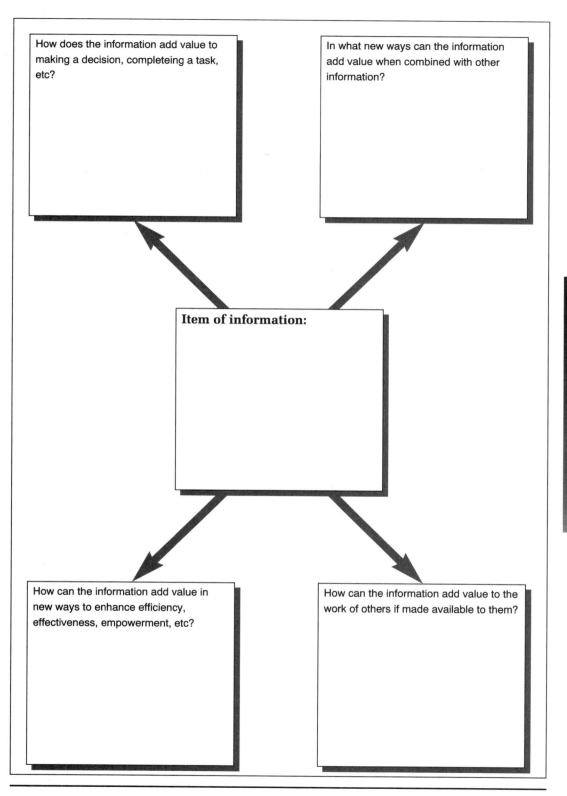

How does the information add value to making a decision, completeing a task, etc?

In what new ways can the information add value when combined with other information?

Item of information:

How can the information add value in new ways to enhance efficiency, effectiveness, empowerment, etc?

How can the information add value to the work of others if made available to them?

Step 3: How Can I Get It?

In a fast-moving world quick access to the information you need is crucial. Use the diagram below to help you assess how quickly you can get the information you want by:

- assessing what barriers exist to getting the information you want – for example, lack of authority, compatibility problems, communication problems
- finding ways to overcome those barriers.

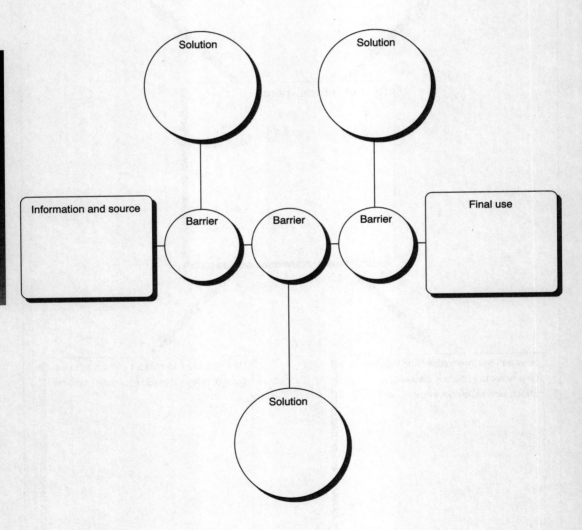

Step 4: When Do I Need It?

Plan the timing of the arrival of the information you need by constructing a diagram similar to that below. Alter the length of the incoming information arrows to represent the time it will take to get the information in time.

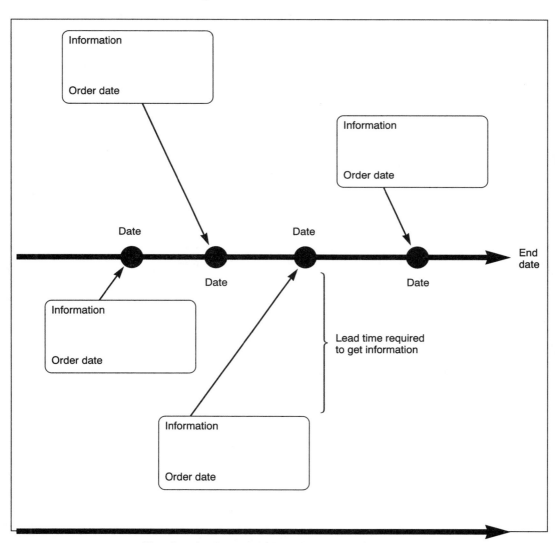

Time line of project or decision process

Step 5: In What Form Do I Need It?

Make sure that you receive information in a form that is most useful to you by establishing the correct criteria at the outset. Use the diagram below to help you.

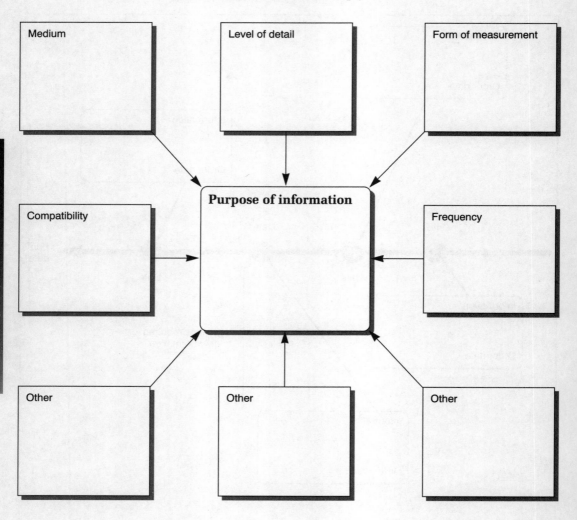

You can't expect others to give you what you want if you don't explain it to them clearly. Make the process of gathering data a useful exercise in communication within your team – do they know why you want the information, what you will do with it and what value it will add? Armed with this knowledge they will be able to help you much more effectively.

Step 6: Who Else Needs It?

Make sure that the information you pass on is of greater value or use than when you received it by completing the diagram below.

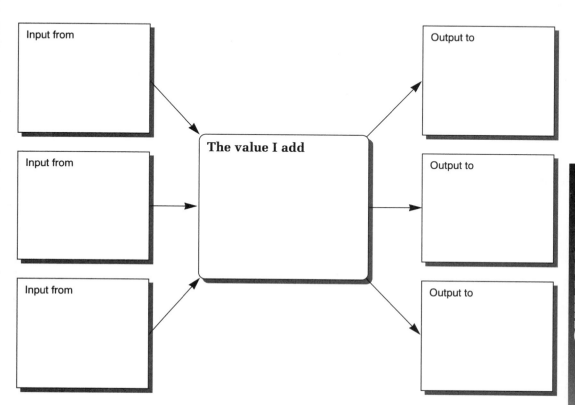

An important way you can add value is by communicating information clearly. Write down in the box below what you can do to pass information on in the most easily absorbed way – for example, by using graphs, diagrams, and so on.

Never be afraid to ask the dumb questions – they're usually the ones that most need to be asked!

Step 7: How Can I Better Meet The Needs of Others and Myself?

Make sure that the information which you pass on meets others' needs. You can only do this by knowing why the information is needed from you. If you don't know or don't fully understand, **ask**!

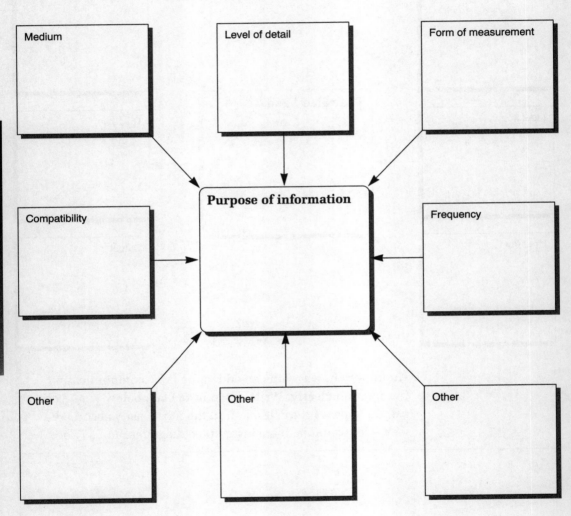

Medium

Level of detail

Form of measurement

Compatibility

Purpose of information

Frequency

Other

Other

Other

Your Information Audit

The following table summarizes the key questions to ask when conducting your information audit.

PURPOSE

1. Why do I need it?

To prevent yourself being overwhelmed you must be ruthless in assessing the value of each piece of data. Unless it directly contributes to achieving a specific objective, reject it.

Can I achieve my objective without this data? If your answer is 'yes' – reject it.

2. How will I use it?

You must know how you will use a piece of information before accepting it.

How will this information help me achieve my objective?
How will it link to other pieces of information?
How will it enhance the value of other information?
How can it be used in entirely new ways to add value?

ACCESSIBILITY

3. How can I get it?

To achieve an objective you need to secure your access paths to information.

Do I know where this information is?
Do I have the authority to access it?

4. When do I need it?

Information which arrives too early can be a distraction. Information which arrives too late can be a disaster.

How long will it take to get it?
At what stage does it form a crucial input into achieving my objective?

5. In what form do I need it?

To be useful, information must come in the right form.

What criteria do I need to set for receiving information?
What compatibility problems may arise?
In what way do I intend to interpret the information?

COMMUNICATION

6. Who else needs it?

The outcome of your activities forms the inputs to someone else's activities. To be effective you must be able to communicate with them.

Who are the links in my activity chain?
How am I adding value to what I pass on to them?
What is the most effective way of communicating with them?

EVALUATION

7. How can I better meet the needs of others and myself?

Other people should be completing their own information audit. You need to link up with them to maximize synergy and compatibility and review constantly for improvement.

What can I do to further improve the information that others receive from me?
How can I further improve my own systems?

CHECK POINTS

ACTION POINTS

Use this framework to conduct your own information audits.

PURPOSE

1. Why do I need it?	2. How will I use it?

ACCESSIBILITY

3. How can I get it?	4. When do I need it?	5. In what form do I need it?

COMMUNICATION

6. Who else needs it?

EVALUATION

7. How can I better meet the needs of others and myself?

CHECK POINTS

PART II

Using IT For Competitiveness

Part II will show you how to:

- control the flows of information needed to do your job
- organize your workspaces to take best advantage of new technologies
- use IT to maintain coordination and cooperation in decentralized organizations
- control the amount of serendipity needed in your job
- create time to think and be with people – depressurizing the workplace.

Introduction

Information technology is shifting the battle for competitive advantage from the physical marketplace to the rapidly evolving market**space** where the winners will be those people who can make the best use of information resources. In marketspace physical distance, as a barrier to interaction, is irrelevant. The global IT network makes everywhere and everyone equally accessible. The implications of this for the way we structure and operate businesses and organizations are enormous.

Information technology is vital to competitiveness in two ways:

- IT offers the means to coordinate activities within increasingly dispersed organizations by providing the essential real-time conduits for communication and information flow through the creation of intranets. Dispersed organizations cannot function competitively without excellent communication. The development of intranets makes the dispersed, 'virtual' organization viable.
- IT forms the framework within which the marketspace exists and therefore gives organizations the ability to generate competitive advantage through the limitless added-value opportunities which IT presents.

Creating Your Workspace for Competing in the Marketspace

In this unit you will work towards:

- controlling the information that flows across your desk
- creating a workspace that fits with the use of modern technology
- using IT so that your desk is with you wherever you are.

Managing Data Inflows

Many managers are at sea in oceans of data. Determining what is useful takes too much time, is distracting and prevents effective action. One of the ways round this is to maximize the use of IT to minimize unwanted data.

Where are you?

- Drowning – overboard – can you reach a lifeline?
- Feeling seasick – can you make your way to a port or are you so preoccupied with staying afloat that you don't know where you're going?

• On the island? Don't be complacent – advances in technology are so rapid that you can easily be left behind.

The diagram below illustrates some of the sources of inflowing data. To control the flow you should put effective filters in place to intercept unwanted data. These filters may be, for example:

• vetting, and removal from, unnecessary mailing and circulation lists
• a secretary
• colleagues
• your own self-discipline.

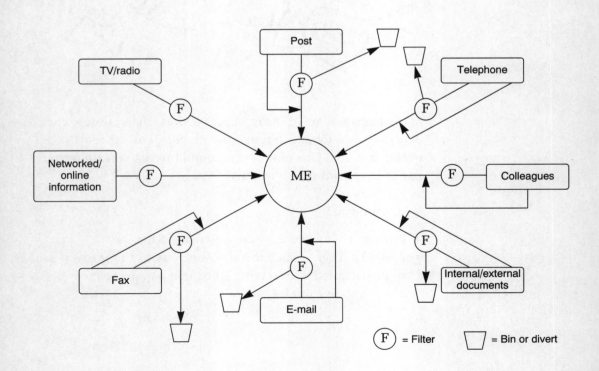

96

Managing Data Outflows

It is equally important to consider your outflow of information to others – colleagues, bosses, suppliers, customers and so on. Do you swamp them with more information than they need or want?

Control your outflows. Put in filters to check that your outflows will be worthwhile to others. Always ask the questions:

- Am I adding value and helping others?
- Am I clogging up the system with unnecessary communication?
- Am I being an effective team player?

Remember – **it all has to be read by someone!**

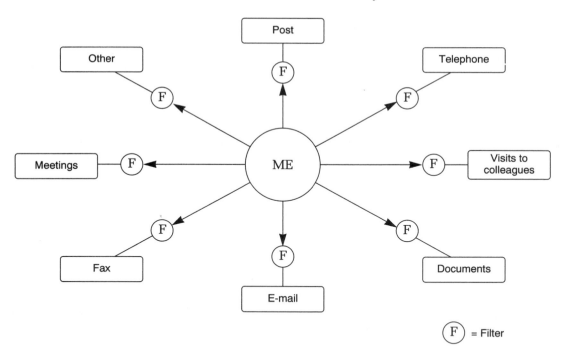

Stemming the Flow of Paper and Organizing Information Flow and Retrieval

If you have analysed your information inflows and outflows you will have set filters in place to reduce the flows to what is useful and necessary. If the flows that remain are largely paper-based you should now assess how much of the information communicated on paper could be dealt with more effectively by using IT.

We all have a problem here – the paperless office has been predicted for at least the last 20 years, but the very reverse has been the case. Why? We like paper and feel comfortable with it because we generally prefer high touch, low tech solutions – things we can touch and feel. Paper is very convenient and user-friendly – you take it anywhere and use it anyhow. But it is like any other drug – used in moderation or correctly prescribed, it can do you a power of good, but an overdose may kill you!

The problem is that we work in very fluid environments but the information contained on paper is static. You cannot pick the words up off the page and rearrange or change them. This is fine if you're reading a Shakespeare play, but most of us don't work with Shakespeare plays. If the information is static it's out-of-date and useless – **information is dynamic**.

---

*I*nsight: **CUTTING COSTS NOT TREES**

In one company the weekly branch letter to all retail managers used to be sent as a paper document. This meant delivering a 10-page document to 400 sites and amounted to approximately 4000 pages per week or over 200 000 pages per year. Think of the costs of production and distribution! Now the document is e-mailed to all sites simultaneously – no paper, no photocopying, almost no cost, and the information gets there faster. Another advantage is that managers can respond to Head Office just as quickly. They can give immediate feedback, enabling more informed, flexible responses. This is what gives a company competitive edge.

YOU MAY NOW CONTINUE WITH THE NEXT FAST TRACK SECTION ON PAGE 99
OR MOVE TO THE SKILLBUILDER EXERCISE ON PAGES 111–112

Getting to Grips With Your Office and Desk

Once you have gained control of your information flows, you need to tackle your own working space. Become a model successful manager in the information age. Operate as an agent for change and promote more effective ways of working.

Don't be afraid to attempt new modes of working – others will follow if they work. You may not be able to change the way your whole organization operates at once, but you can make a start with yourself and your immediate team.

Be alert to new effective ways of operating:

- Read the press, particularly the *Times* and *Financial Times* which often run supplements on the use of information technology in business and at work.
- Visit exhibitions to see what's new and potentially useful. Don't be taken in by the hype, but don't let it blinker you either.
- Look out for new hardware and software that will free you to do more. If a machine can take over some tasks, let go and either do more or start something new. Be more effective; add more value.
- Observe your colleagues. Notice how others, both inside and outside your company, work – emulate, copy and adapt their good working practices and drop the bad ones.
- Above all, choose what works well for you and those with whom you interact. It makes no sense to adopt a technology or way of working that does not suit you, your colleagues, your organization and your customers.

BENEFITING FROM THE APPROPRIATE USE OF IT

There is one fundamental benefit of the appropriate use of IT:

THE TIME TO MANAGE

By reducing the time you spend on processing and handling information, you have more time to spend on:

- **walking** the floor
- **talking** to people
- **making** decisions
- **taking** action
- **contributing**, adding value and being effective.

> Information is only a resource – a means to an end – it is not the job itself. Use IT to manage the information, while you get on with the job.

Turning Molehills into Anthills: Changing the Mindset

Go to the ant, thou sluggard. Learn her ways and be wise.
(Proverbs 6:6)

If your office is more like a molehill than an anthill, what are you going to do about it? You need to plan a new office environment making the optimum use of IT, but this is often where the problems start . . .

IT is like pornography – initially exciting, ultimately disappointing. (Anon)

If this is your experience (of IT, not pornography!) then you may have experienced some of the typical problems associated with IT – for example:

- limitations of your office wiring and communications system.
- constraints on cordlessness and portability of equipment
- disappointments relating to experiences with teleconferencing
- inadequate and inhuman interfaces
- multiple devices which can't work together. (*We constantly hear about the need for teamwork among our colleagues – what about some teamwork among the equipment!*)
- inadequate storage and processing power
- people who do not respond to change and block the system.

But, as the examples opposite show, such is IT's current level of flexibility and sophistication that most of these barriers no longer exist. The development of organizational intranets means that where you work becomes irrelevant because access to information becomes ubiquitous.

Insight: HOT DESKING – YOUR OFFICE ON WHEELS

A London-based publishing company has replaced the old fixed-space office concept with something more fluid that fits better with the way its staff work – as teams that come together and disperse as necessary. It decided that it was time to get the office furniture on the move as well as people. With uniform hardware and software throughout the company anyone can plug in anywhere, wheeling their office desk to where it suits them and others most. Everyone has a mobile phone linked to a switchboard with a radio transmitter that reaches beyond the building: answering the switchboard is everyone's responsibility. In addition to the benefits of flexible working, there have been cost savings too. There is less need for everyone to have the highest-specification machines. Instead, those who need high-power computing only occasionally can move around to find it. (Financial Times, *1 November 1995)*

Insight: NO OFFICE AT ALL – YOU ARE YOUR OWN OFFICE

In the most advanced companies the concept of the office is disappearing altogether. There are workspaces and meeting rooms – people carry their office with them in the car, train, plane, hotel and home, as well as in company buildings. All the resources we need can now be carried or worn. The resources you cannot carry are all around you and usable – copiers, fax, printers, chairs, tables and coffee pots! The old office paradigm was about identity, status and territory. The new paradigm is about information, access and communication. Respect and status then become products of contribution and effectiveness.

Building a Better Anthill

The key to success in building a successful IT-based office is to make sure that all the systems you put in place **Integrate** with each other.

THE SOLUTION NOW

The telegram, letter, fax, telephone, voicemail and paper have all served us well and brought about tremendous change and productivity gains. But they have drawbacks.

- The letter is too slow for any modern business.
- The fax is often of dubious quality.
- A telephone demands that we answer it, and is becoming more useful as a mobile device.

But now there are new contenders:

- **e-mail**
- **electronic file transfer**
- **networking**.

These are more immediate, convenient and faster tools for much of our work.

What we have to do is choose the right channel and technology for our purpose. Using IT – from word processing, spreadsheets, accounting packages through to business card readers – to maximum advantage adds to our individual effectiveness.

The advantages of electronic mail

- No secretary, paper, envelopes, stamps, postman – no delay!
- Immediate, succinct, international, convenient.
- Bypasses managers and hierarchies – helps to change organizations!
- Does not have to be location-specific – you can access it on the move!

Curiously, e-mail reinstates delay and is simultaneously more responsive – an interesting mid-point solution!

The advantages of information networking – intranets

- On-screen working is not passive but interactive – a place for animation!
- Fast and comprehensive with less clutter – can create more understanding!
- Easier to store, carry and file – it can always be with you!

Working on the Run

If you work in a dynamic organization it is crucial to spend time with people and, for many managers, this means travelling the globe. But because you are on the move does not mean you have to be away from the office! Those car, train and plane journeys and those nights in hotels represent valuable time to be exploited.

With a laptop, a modem, connectors, cables and crocodile clips, plus screwdrivers, you can be online from anywhere. With a GSM phone you can be online on the move! Your laptop then becomes your office and the building blocks are essentially simple and a facsimile of your fixed office!

Remember – IT enables us to be effective anytime, anywhere . . . literally!

- **Mobile phone:** Allows you to use your 'down time' when in the car, walking and travelling! Network services now provide automatic call diversion, call-back, messaging and answering machine facilities.
- **Dictaphone:** You can capture ideas, draft letters and memos while stuck in traffic! You can record meetings and presentations for later transcription! You can rehearse verbal arguments and phrases ahead of time!
- **Laptops:** Your office can always be with you – always on your shoulder! With a good collection of connectors and a portable modem you can get online from anywhere in the world! A small set of screwdrivers and crocodile clips are also essential!
- **Video conferencing:** The technology for video conferencing to the desk is readily available – it may seem expensive, but if you compare its cost to even the most modest trip in terms of travelling, hotel, time, fatigue and effectiveness for each individual involved, it looks cheaper by the minute!

Admittedly, you will need an ISDN line to achieve a reasonable working quality of sound and picture but, again, the expense is trivial compared to the equivalent cost, of time and travel.

YOU MAY NOW CONTINUE WITH THE NEXT FAST TRACK SECTION ON PAGE 105 OR MOVE TO THE SKILLBUILDER EXERCISE ON PAGE 118

The Solution Tomorrow – or Very Soon After

If you feel overwhelmed by the technological choices open to you today, then stand by for more. Within the next two years there will be a myriad new devices, software and services. Not only will there be more of the same – more powerful PCs, faster LANs, more capable software – there will also be novel developments which pose new challenges:

- combined PC/games console/television/hi-fi/modems for the home
- combined laptop PC/organizer/GSM phone/pager, that you carry or wear
- cordless LANs which eliminate the need for office wiring
- text-to-speech and speech-to-text applications
- automatic translation between languages
- text précis of written texts
- better search engines for the Internet
- agent technologies which provide the first artificial intelligence support
- standard software/application blocks that we can knit together to meet our specific business and life needs
- global positioning for vehicles and people – where are you and where are they?
- video conferencing that really works
- security and identification through biometrics
- new mobile systems for digital communication between people and machines
- new high-definition displays.

The longer you wait to adopt the new ways of working and managing with IT, the further you are going to be left behind. The message has to be 'get with it or you'll be without' – without the business or the organization!

*I*nsight: THE PC IS DEAD, LONG LIVE THE NETWORK PC?

The development of the Internet may spell the end of the PC as we know it. Sun Microsystems see the future as belonging to network computers which use software stored on the Internet instead of on the PC's hard disk. This gives the network PC potentially unlimited access to the most up-to-date software as and when you need it.

*I*nsight: EARLY WARNING

If you work in a paper-intensive organization which you consider chaotic and if you are overwhelmed by information, just wait until you go electronic and start networking. You can look forward to a world of unimaginable potential information mountains!

Merely moving the paper from the desk top to the screen will not work well. Your output will go up by tenfold in a decade and the information flow involved will be magnified by hundreds. Of course, computers can search and find rapidly – but only if you have been disciplined in categorizing information at the front end.

For those who have been screen-centric for a decade, it is interesting to look back and remember the escalation of RAM and the hard disk! Many of us started with 40 Mbyte, and then rapidly moved up to 80, 120, 250, 500, 1000, and now 2000 Mbyte hard disks and more. What have we done with all this space? Well, the temptation is to keep everything and, of course, you can, but it costs money and can create confusion. You have to choose! How do you want to live?

YOU MAY NOW CONTINUE WITH THE NEXT FAST TRACK SECTION ON PAGE 123

Managing Data Inflows

Use the chart below to assess and manage your current data inflow.

- Write in each square category box those flows you want to control.
- Write in each circular filter box the filter you will establish to stop the unwanted data.

If you have additional inflows that you need to monitor, you can add further boxes.

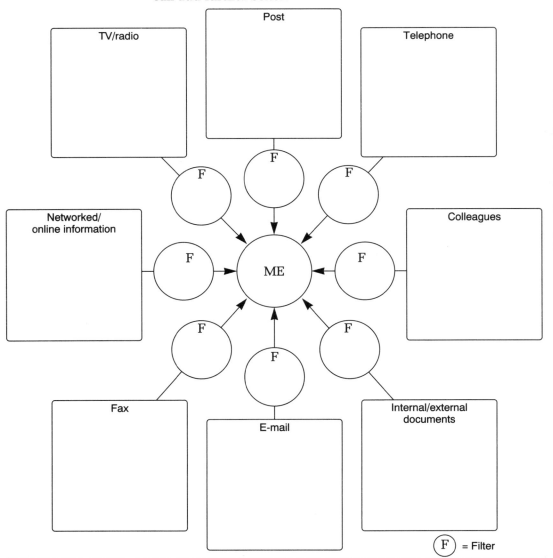

Monitor the flow from each source for a day or week before and after you put working filters in place. Use the following chart to monitor your progress.

Inflow	Before			After		
	% total input	% useful input	% of my time taken	% total input	% useful input	% of my time taken
Post						
Telephone						
Colleagues						
Int/ext. docs						
E-mail						
Fax						
Online info						
TV/radio						
Other						

What improvements have you achieved?

SKILLBUILDER

Managing Data Outflows

Use the chart below to assess and manage your current data outflow.

- Write in each square category box those flows you don't consider really necessary.
- Write in each circular filter box the filter you will establish to stop the unwanted flow.

If you have additional outflows that you need to monitor, you can add further boxes.

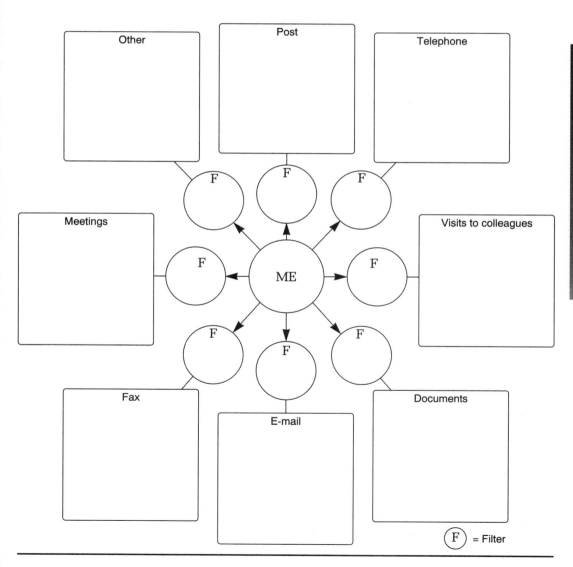

Monitor the flow from each source for a day or week before and after you put working filters in place. Use the following chart to monitor your progress. Ask colleagues to monitor your progress as well.

	Before			After		
Outflow	**% total output**	**% useful output**	**% of my time taken**	**% total output**	**% useful output**	**% of my time taken**
Post						
Telephone						
Colleagues						
Docs						
E-mail						
Fax						
Meetings						
Other						
Other						

What improvements have you achieved?

SKILLBUILDER

Stemming the Flow of Paper and Organizing Information Flow and Retrieval

Review all the work you do that is paper-based and decide whether paper is the most appropriate medium or whether there are more effective alternatives. For example, why use written memos when you can send an e-mail? Why have an overflowing Filofax, when you could have an electronic organizer?

Use the table below to assess your current paper usage and devise viable, alternative, IT-based ways of working. If there are barriers to adopting these new methods, describe them and seek ways to eliminate them.

Type of paper-based information	Alternative IT means of communication	Current significant barriers to change – technical or human	Possible ways of overcoming the barriers

Now analyse your results:

1. Those areas for which there is an IT alternative with no significant barriers are *areas in which you can take action now. DO IT.*
2. Those areas for which IT can provide an effective alternative but for which there are significant barriers to overcome (either technical or relating to individuals, such as a manager who has never used a PC and can't see its advantages) are *areas where you need to action a plan to overcome the barrier. Draw up a plan NOW.*
3. For those areas for which you can see no IT alternative, *first, check that your IT knowledge is up-to-date. If there is still no IT solution then what you have left is the residual information for which paper is the best medium. Look for ways to cut down on words by using diagrams and graphs (see Unit 3, page 54).*

SKILLBUILDER

Getting to Grips With Your Office and Desk

Take a Polaroid picture of your office as it looks towards the end of a working day – say at 5.00 pm. Don't cheat by tidying up beforehand or choosing a day when you haven't had a chance to make a mess. When your picture is developed, compare it to the two photographs on this page. Which does your office most closely resemble?

Does your office resemble a molehill – a disorganized heap of machines, paper, telephone, fax, filing cabinets? Is yours an office environment where information and information technology are poorly utilized and managed?

Alternatively, does your office resemble an anthill – a structured, organized working environment with a clean office/desk, one machine, camera, scanner, telephone, very little paper – an environment where information and information technology are well utilized and managed?

What is the fundamental difference between the two? Less paper. In which office will you be able to work smarter rather than harder?

However, you should also be happy with the way your office or desk is organized. If you're constantly frustrated, you cannot work smarter.

Overleaf we present a wish list. Test yourself and your colleagues to find out what your wishes are. The more you have, the greater your level of frustration and the greater the spur to do something about it.

I wish . . .	Me	Colleague 1	Colleague 2	Colleague 3
my phone was always with me				
my desk wasn't covered with cables and machines				
I could find people when I want them and they could find me				
I could get rid of all this paper				
I didn't have to travel so much				
I could be in two places at once				
my PC wasn't so slow and unfriendly				
I could talk to my PC and it to me				
my diary and schedule were automatic and up-to-date				
I had an automatic database of all my contacts				
my mail was electronically sorted, summarized, prioritized and filed				
information could be retrieved with only a partial description				
I could voice-annotate documents				
I had all the power of my office wherever I was				

SKILLBUILDER

Turning Molehills into Anthills – Overcoming the Barriers to Change

Use the table below to identify your barriers and seek ways to circumvent them. We have listed some of the most common from the previous page but you can add others of your own.

Barrier	Solution
Limitations of your office wiring and communications system	
Constraints on cordlessness and portability of equipment	
Disappointments relating to experiences with teleconferencing	
Inadequate and inhuman interfaces	
Multiple devices which can't work together	
Inadequate storage and processing power	
People who do not respond to change and block the system	

SKILLBUILDER

Building a Better Anthill: What to Do and How to Do It!

An electronic network is an absolute essential. You need solid, tried and tested hardware and software, but most of all you need the technical skills to get it all working.

Do not try to do it all yourself by reading handbooks – *your life will run out before you make it!* Employ specialist people to build your integrated, electronic environment.

You can purchase off-the-shelf local area networks, servers and Internet access almost as easily as you can buy jelly beans! Getting them all to work well together is another matter! Plug and play is still something of a dream – consult an expert! But watch, listen and learn – don't be a technophobe, become a technophile because it is the future and a means of increasing your value. You may not be, nor ever become, an expert but you do need to understand and to be able to speak the language!

WHAT YOU NEED

Use the table opposite to plan your IT environment. Multi-function machines will increasingly reduce the number of boxes on your desk. For example, Hewlett-Packard and Xerox are introducing machines which combine colour copying and printing and it won't be long before your computer combines fax, e-mail, printer, copier and scanner functions. What you carry will also be revolutionized: combined organizer–digital mobile phones are just coming on to the market and will be soon followed by the combined laptop–telephone. Being online is becoming easier!

Equipment	What can I do?
The best PC you can afford	
A printer shared by the office	
A fax – perhaps! You can fax from/into a PC, so why replicate? It is now possible to get a fax/PC/printer combined	
A scanner to transfer all incoming paper on-screen	
A copier – but remember that a scanner and printer can sometimes do the same job!	
A back-up machine to cache or vault all that vital data – better to have multiple storage locations in case a disk crash destroys everything	
A CD burner to capture complete tranches of work	
Software that serves your business needs: • word processing • spreadsheet • graphics • e-mail • networking	
A telephone system that works – use network services such as transfer, answerphone, recall etc. to best advantage	

SKILLBUILDER

Working on the Run

Use the table below to plan your mobile IT environment.

Equipment	What can I do?
Mobile phone	
Network services with automatic call diversion, call-back, messaging and answering machine facilities	
Dictaphone	
Laptop	
The kit to get you online worldwide	
Video conferencing	
A GSM phone	
Battery packs	

Remember – take advice. Observe and talk to as many people as possible before you buy.

Using a charge card considerably reduces your hotel telephone bill.

In the hotel and office, the fax machine can be used to give you hard copy when there is no printer available.

On long flights you will need extra battery packs for your laptop – although you can charge up from the razor socket in the toilet, the airlines don't like it! Soon, however, airlines will have seat sockets into which you can plug your laptop and send and receive information to and from your office via newly established ground stations.

Although GSM works over most of Europe, the standards are different in the USA. Although you can hire units – a fixed line is cheaper.

Software that automatically dials in, logs into your mail system, downloads and uploads is well worth the investment.

SKILLBUILDER

Creating Your Workspace for Competing in the Marketplace

To win you have to:

- be prepared to change the way you think, work and organize your life
- be determined to eradicate as much paper as possible
- be persistent in getting the technology to do your bidding
- try to convince others to adopt the same paradigm
- experiment with every aspect of your working and non-working lives
- choose what works and abandon what does not
- watch the leaders and follow technology developments
- talk to as many people as possible to share experiences, problems and solutions
- constantly question and challenge the status quo
- redefine the role of the secretary and everyone else – what new tasks will the technology allow them to do?
- be prepared to invest your time and money to effect positive change.

Remember: the biggest benefit of IT is

the time to manage.

ACTION POINTS

As a summary to this unit:

1. Write your own information management plan, maximizing the appropriate use of IT, for your office, fixed desk and mobile desk.
2. Present your plan to your colleagues and then to your manager and gain approval, if you need it, to action the three most important points.

Your plan should show the potential to benefit you, your colleagues, your manager and the organization. You can use the table overleaf to help you begin.

CHECK POINTS

MANAGING INFORMATION: ACTION PLAN NO. 3
PUTTING IT TO WORK

Controlling data flows	
Transforming the work environment	
Communicating with IT	
Making the office transportable	
Making more time to be with people	
Adding more value to data-creating information	
Dumping all that rubbish	

IT: The Centre of CompetITiveness

In this unit you will:

- identify your organization's position in terms of coordination and decentralization and the impact of this on the use of IT
- consider how IT can help you manage people more effectively
- consider how IT can help you manage time more effectively
- consider how IT can help you create marketspace opportunities.

Coordination versus Decentralization: 1

Modern organizations are often characterized by flatter structures and more independent and empowered units. These may consist of project teams which form and disperse as the organization's needs change. In this type of environment there is a tension between decentralization and coordination – **this should be a creative tension.**

As business strategy drives towards increasing decentralization the need for coordination increases if a coherent strategy is to be maintained.

---

*I*nsight: **GOING GLOBAL**

Ford Motors moved from marketplace to marketspace when they set about designing their new global car. To design such a car, Ford wanted to pool the best engineering, design and marketing talents from all its operations worldwide. In the

---

past this would have required enormously costly meetings, in terms of time and money, to bring everyone together. Instead, Ford created, via its own intranet, a virtual team to develop the car that was spread worldwide but connected through the computer network.

In addition to the cost and time savings the benefits included the added value gained by working in marketspace – for example, the ability to work on the project 24 hours a day as work was passed around the world, the ability for individuals to work together sharing documents and designs in real time while separated by thousands of miles and, above all, through the creation of a complete information-based representation of the product, the ability of everyone on the team to see the project as a whole. A global team could create a global car with global appeal – and all without moving an inch! (Harvard Business Review, *73 (6), 1995, 75–85*)

YOU MAY NOW CONTINUE WITH THE NEXT FAST TRACK SECTION ON PAGE 125 OR MOVE TO THE SKILLBUILDER EXERCISE ON PAGE 135

Coordination versus Decentralization: 2

The four types of organization management identified in the diagram below will display very different attitudes and approaches towards information management:

1. **Centralized:** characterized by tight control, the predomination of top-down flows and the restriction of information on a need-to-know basis.

   The democratic flow of information produced by IT has serious implications for the management of such organizations. Tensions may become intolerable.

2. **Integrated:** characterized by two-way, free flow of information through a network.

   Such organizations are probably highly receptive to innovations made possible through IT. IT will fit well into, and help to strengthen, the organization.

3. **Unintegrated:** characterized by poorly controlled top-down flow where those who need to know may not and those who don't might know.

   If an IT strategy can be implemented, the potential for improving the flow of information may be enormous in this environment.

4. **Disintegrated:** characterized by restricted flows of information among often disconnected and competing parts of the organization.

   In this environment IT might make matters worse if each unit pursues its own independent strategy. The ability of the different parts to communicate may diminish rather than increase.

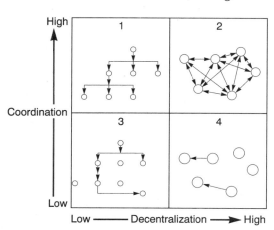

Waves of Decentralization

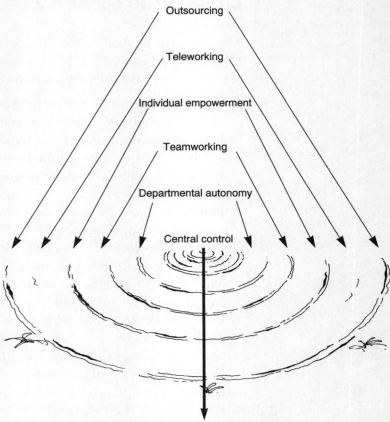

Outsourcing

Teleworking

Individual empowerment

Teamworking

Departmental autonomy

Central control

Increasing decentralization

Decentralization can be visualized as a wave moving out from the centre. Its advantages in terms of enhanced competitiveness are perceived as those of increasing responsiveness and flexibility. However, these advantages are lost if excellent communication is not maintained between all parts of the organization.

In other words, **communication** is the third element of competitiveness.

Ford Motors could not have designed a global car using a globally dispersed team without the means to coordinate everyone's activities. The task depended on the ability of every team member to keep in close touch with each other in real time.

YOU MAY NOW CONTINUE WITH THE NEXT FAST TRACK SECTION ON PAGE 127 OR MOVE TO THE SKILLBUILDER EXERCISE ON PAGES 137–138

Placing IT at the Centre of Competitiveness: 1 – People

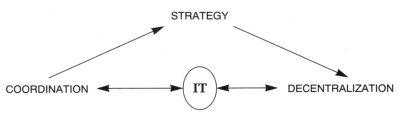

Managing the tension between coordination and decentralization positively to enhance competitiveness depends on your ability to communicate. However, traditional modes of communication come under increasing strain, and many become irrelevant and inappropriate, as decentralization increases. The tendency is for people to become swamped by more and more paper and bureaucracy and to spend increasing time in, and travelling to, meetings.

One solution is to adopt a wider range of communication approaches including appropriate IT to create an effective communications hub that holds the ring between coordination and decentralization.

Using IT appropriately does not mean abandoning the human touch – on the contrary, it enhances it by:

- creating more time for yourself at work
- creating more time for the people you work with and for those who work for you
- being able to communicate efficiently and effectively with anyone, anywhere
- enabling everyone to work together cooperatively no matter where they are.

What does all this add up to? Increased competitiveness, because the most valuable resource in your organization is the talents of your people in terms of their knowledge, expertise and motivation.

*I*nsight: DOING WHAT WE DO BEST

An area manager at Lincoln, the insurance company, was concerned that the self-image of individual members of his sales team did not fit the reality of what they did best.

Through the IT systems available, the area manager was able to analyse the performance of individual sales managers in terms of how they spent their time and where they won their business. He found that individual salespeople did not always play to their strengths. For example, some young salespeople, who tended to see themselves as up-and-coming financial wizards, spent a great deal of time trying to sell complex investment products to sophisticated older clients who regarded them as inexperienced. In contrast, there were some older salespeople who felt that young couples benefited from their experience. Their young clients, however, felt that these salespeople did not understand their lifestyle and the financial services required to support it.

The area manager used this information as the basis of a training programme to reorientate the sales team into doing what each member really did best for the benefit of their clients, themselves and the company.

YOU MAY NOW CONTINUE WITH THE NEXT FAST TRACK SECTION ON PAGE 129
OR MOVE TO THE SKILLBUILDER EXERCISE ON PAGES 139–140

Placing IT at the Centre of Competitiveness: 2 – Time

One product of decentralization and the globalization of the world economy is the need to work and communicate at a distance. This has resulted in the exponential rise in business travel. Not only do many people waste enormous amounts of their productive time and energy in commuting, when they are at work many will spend even more time in business-related travel – or, rather, waiting to travel.

The cost of business travel to organizations in terms of their employees' wasted time and energy is vast and growing. Organizations which aim to be more competitive will naturally want to use this time more effectively. IT helps to do this by:

- cutting down on unproductive travelling time, both business and commuting
- enabling people to use the time saved doing effective work and communicating across any distance
- enabling those who do have to travel to take their office with them and remain effective while in transit.

*I*nsight: TWENTIETH-CENTURY NOMADS

*The only people who like to travel are those who don't do it!
A typical trip from the UK to the USA can be broken down as
follows:*

ACTIVITY	TIME (HOURS)
Getting to the airport	*2*
Checking in	*2*
Delays	*1*
Baggage reclaim	*0.5*
Customs/security	*0.5*
Ground transport – leaving airport	*1*
Total (non-air travel)	***7** (1 standard working day)*
Flying time	*7*
Total	***14** (2 standard working days)*

*This represents a great deal of ineffective time – it is the
'down time' of life. A trip with a two-hour flight time is even
worse in terms of the proportion of waiting time to travel
time!*

*IT can cut down travel in the same way as the computer can
transform the paper-filled office.*

*I*nsight: TELEPHONE OUTPERFORMS CAR

*In 1956 a telephone call from
the UK to the USA cost £2.80
per minute, in 1995 it cost £0.40
and in 1996 only £0.30. In
contrast it costs £0.44 per mile
to drive a car and, at an average
speed of 60 mph, that's £0.44 per minute!*

Placing IT at the Centre of Your Communication Strategy

With the enormous growth of communication using IT and its rapidly decreasing costs, there are a whole range of practical steps you can take to use IT to increase your competitiveness.

AUDIO CONFERENCING

Audio conferencing using a loudspeaking telephone unit can be a very effective medium for meetings between multiple locations. The equipment, service and calls are an insignificant cost compared to any other alternative and the salaries and time of the people involved.

Sending printed pages, slides/OHP, videos and physical artefacts to all the meeting points so that all parties can view the same material simultaneously at very low cost can considerably enhance audio conferencing.

COMBINING THE INTERNET AND TELEPHONE SERVICES

Combining the Internet and telephone services is also a powerful means of avoiding travel. It enables you to work with good quality audio with files and pictures transferred in delayed time via the Internet. This in turn can be enhanced with multiple telephone lines and the ISDN to give near real-time facilities.

VIDEO CONFERENCING

'Let your mouse do the walking' – use video conferencing from desk top to desk top to cut out wasteful travel. You can hold a team meeting with a group spread all over the world and discuss and actually work on a document or set of plans visible on each individual's machine without anyone having to leave their desk.

BUSINESS TV

The combination of satellite technology and IT allows live TV-style programmes to be fed down to groups of employees and provides a stimulating, informative alternative to, for example, the staid company magazine. Furthermore, it can be produced much more quickly and just as economically with a much greater impact.

EDI (ELECTRONIC DATA INTERCHANGE)

EDI is already well established in a number of industries, notably retailing. It provides instant access to information from computer to computer and permits the automatic handling of a number of supplier–buyer transactions, such as orders, delivery notes and invoices, without incurring the time and cost of paper transactions. The potential for EDI, however, extends much further by enabling close collaboration by different organizations on common-interest projects.

Insight: WHICH CENTURY ARE YOU IN?

A high street bank in a recent 'forward thinking' reorganization of its human resources (HR) function discarded their centralized HR function and introduced roving HR managers to travel around branches. This not only represents a nineteenth-century rather than a twenty-first century mindset, but also an inefficient use of resources. An HR manager can visit a branch just as effectively via the computer screen or even meet groups of branch managers while each remains in their branch. He or she can visit more branches in a day using IT rather than a car! It is time to make intelligent use of IT rather than unintelligent use of the car.

YOU MAY NOW CONTINUE WITH THE NEXT FAST TRACK SECTION ON PAGE 133 OR MOVE TO THE SKILLBUILDER EXERCISE ON PAGE 143

Using IT to Develop Marketspace Opportunities

The example of Interforward below highlights how information technology can transform the ways in which organizations can work together to their mutual benefit as well as create whole new business opportunities.

Insight: **WHAT BUSINESS ARE YOU IN – GOODS OR INFORMATION DISTRIBUTION?**

Interforward is a large goods distribution company which, through the application of EDI, has become an information provider not only to its customers but also to its customers' customers.

Orders for goods distribution are input into Interforward's computer system directly from manufacturers and retailers and are presented on-screen to admin staff with end-user details so that staff can make contact to arrange delivery.

Every action is recorded, providing a complete history of each transaction. All proof of delivery documents are scanned in and stored as images on optical disks. They are available for viewing online (no more hunting through box files).

A significant added-value element of this process is that, by opening it up to its customers, Interforward has slashed the number of enquiries and disputes it handles. Customers can now key into Interforward's system, view the current status of their orders and their transaction details and obtain details of proof of delivery documents automatically by fax. This facility has enabled many of Interforward's customers to streamline their own processes.

Interforward is now opening up its system to the customers of its customers so that they can track the progress of their orders much more quickly than going to the manufacturer who would in turn have contacted Interforward. This allows these businesses to plan their own processes more effectively.

As Interforward says, it's the customer's information anyway, so why shouldn't they access it?

This approach shows a radical shift towards the collaborative use of information between businesses that works to everyone's benefit. Once it is realized that the value of information is not diminished by the number of different uses to which it is put, whole new areas of opportunity open up. (Financial Times, 1 November 1995)

*I*nsight: **WHO'S LOOKING AFTER THE ORPHANS?**

In the insurance industry, turnover of sales staff is rapid. This leaves large numbers of clients as 'orphans' with no direct link to the company if their sales contact leaves. Consequently, they tend to lose contact and can fall prey to the competition. To minimize this risk, Lincoln uses its database to identify instantly all the 'orphans' of a departing salesperson and reallocate them immediately. Furthermore, the data available on each client enables Lincoln to identify the most suitable salesperson to foster a relationship with the 'orphan'. This quick and targeted response, made possible by using information effectively, has greatly reduced the loss of 'orphans' and all the potential future business they represent.

YOU MAY NOW CONTINUE WITH THE NEXT FAST TRACK SECTION ON PAGE 149
OR MOVE TO THE SKILLBUILDER EXERCISE ON PAGES 144

Coordination versus Decentralization: 1

It is important to know what type of organization you work in.

Look at the words displayed below and circle the eight which you think **most** apply to your organization.

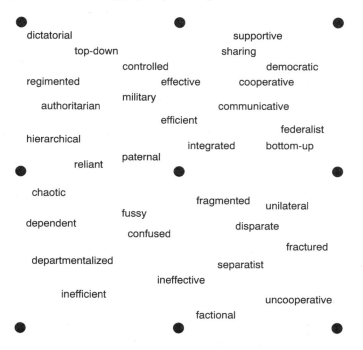

dictatorial
top-down
controlled
regimented
effective
military
authoritarian
efficient
hierarchical
reliant
paternal
chaotic
fussy
dependent
confused
departmentalized
ineffective
inefficient
factional

supportive
sharing
democratic
cooperative
communicative
federalist
integrated
bottom-up
fragmented
unilateral
disparate
fractured
separatist
uncooperative

Then join up the bullet points to form a grid around the collection of words and label it as follows.

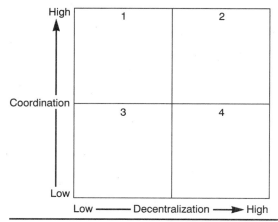

Label each box as follows and total the number of words circled in that box.

Box 1: Centralized   No. of words =
Box 2: Integrated   No. of words =
Box 3: Unintegrated   No. of words =
Box 4: Disintegrated   No. of words =

The box with the most circled words is the one that most accurately describes your organization.

Coordination versus Decentralization: 2

Use the chart below to consider:

- how information is managed in your organization and other types of organization familiar to you
- what the potential impact of introducing IT might be on the flow of information and its effective use in your and other types of organization.

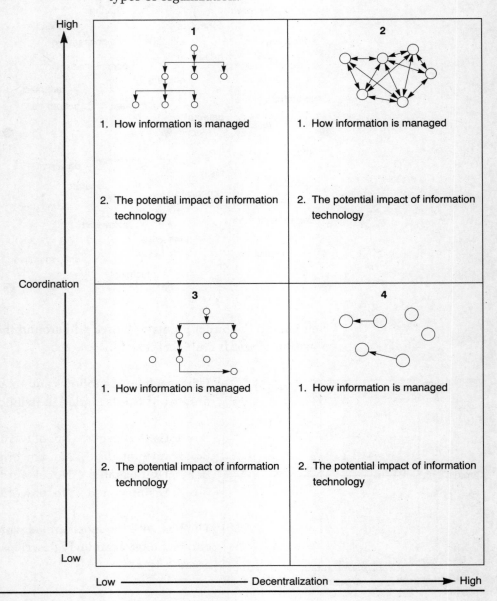

Waves of Decentralization

Use the diagram below for the following tasks:

- Identify the types of decentralization operating in your organization. These may be different or additional to those we have identified.
- Position your organization on the decentralization wave. How far out from the centre have you moved? Place a cross in the appropriate position on the diagram below.
- Assess where your organization will be in one, three and five years' time by drawing an arrow from your present position to your anticipated future ones and labelling each position as one, three and five years.

Note: It is possible that, after going through a period of decentralization, your organization is moving back towards more centralized control. In such a case your path will turn back on itself. If this is true for your organization, you might want to consider why this has happened. Is it a result of a failure in coordination?

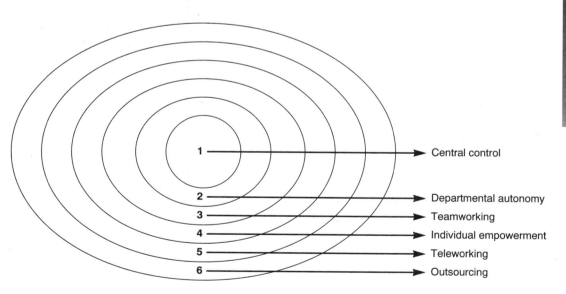

For each of the positions you have located, both current and future, identify the issues of coordination that you believe will develop.

Current: _____

_____

_____

_____

1 year: _____

_____

_____

_____

3 year: _____

_____

_____

_____

5 year: _____

_____

_____

_____

Placing IT at the Centre of Competitiveness: 1 – People

Use the audit below to assess how well your communications support your need for coordination.

COMMUNICATIONS AUDIT

Consider your current job and organization and tick each statement with which you agree.

☐ 1. We do not pool ideas in our department/team.
☐ 2. We don't form alliances with outsiders, like suppliers.
☐ 3. I do not receive sufficient feedback.
☐ 4. Some of our managers are unsupportive.
☐ 5. We do not share skills and information sufficiently.
☐ 6. We seldom work effectively with other teams/departments.
☐ 7. People are unwilling to take the views of others into account.
☐ 8. I do not feel supported by my colleagues.
☐ 9. Team members are insufficiently involved in decision-making.
☐ 10. We seldom transfer people across from other departments to help out with their specialist expertise.
☐ 11. Individuals are not encouraged to develop.
☐ 12. Commitment to decisions is low.
☐ 13. We do not consider alternative solutions sufficiently.
☐ 14. We seldom work effectively with other parts of the organization.
☐ 15. We seldom change our working procedures or organization in response to feedback from others.
☐ 16. People blame others for failures.
☐ 17. People feel frustrated because they are not consulted.
☐ 18. We put a lot of energy into defending our departmental jobs.
☐ 19. People hear what they want to hear, rather than the truth.
☐ 20. We do not try to understand the views of other teams.
☐ 21. Ideas from outside our team are not used.
☐ 22. People should be more independent.
☐ 23. Team members do not receive sufficient honest feedback.
☐ 24. We do not reach out to help other groups.
☐ 25. Different parts of the organization seem to be pulling in different directions.
☐ 26. We do not form informal groups to work on projects or problems.
☐ 27. We do not admit our differences to each other.
☐ 28. We have too little influence on the rest of the organization.
☐ 29. Information does not flow freely enough between teams/departments.
☐ 30. We do not really work together.
☐ 31. We should take more account of how others see us.
☐ 32. There is not enough listening done here.

SKILLBUILDER

Circle all the statement numbers which you ticked in the list below.

P	A	L	S
1	2	3	4
5	6	7	8
9	10	11	12
13	14	15	16
17	18	19	20
21	22	23	24
25	26	27	28
29	30	31	32

Total

Write your scores for each column in the table below. The higher your score in any column the more attention you need to pay to those aspects of communication.

	Score
P (Pooling information)	
F (Forming **A**lliances)	
L (Learning and feedback)	
S (Supporting others)	

For those areas where you score highly, make notes on how you can improve your performance in these areas.

SKILLBUILDER

Placing IT at the Centre of Competitiveness: 2 – Time

Using the table below, log how much of your time is wasted in travel and waiting to travel over a week, month or other suitable period and calculate the associated costs. Include all the time spent waiting to travel – for example, at airports, railway stations and waiting to start meetings. As a working assumption you can cost travel by car at £0.44 per mile.

Time spent	Period 1		Period 2		Period 3	
	Time	Cost	Time	Cost	Time	Cost
Daily commuting						
Waiting to travel						
Actual travel time to meetings within the organization						
Actual travel time to see customers/clients						
Actual travel time to see suppliers						
Other business travel						
Total						

For each period you have recorded, note down what productive activities you could have completed in that time and their value to your organization. Use the example table below to make up your own log sheet.

Alternative productive activities	Period 1		Period 2		Period 3	
	Time	Value	Time	Value	Time	Value
Total						

Sum the total of travel and waiting costs and the total value of the alternative productive activities. This represents the real cost, to your organization, of the travelling you do.

My real cost of travelling: _____

This cost represents a drain on your competitiveness without taking into account any additional social, environmental and personal costs.

To calculate the true impact of your travel on your business, you can deduct the cost of travelling from the value of the business done as a result of the travel.

Value of business done: _____

Value of business done minus real travel cost: _____

Consider how much of this work could have been done by staying in the office and using IT instead. What would be the investment costs of achieving this? How quickly would the reduced travel costs pay for the investment?

Compare the cost of a video conferencing call to achieve the same objective. Take the travel budget and expenditure for a complete year and examine what percentage of work could actually have been avoided or completed by using video and/or audio conferencing. The chances are that you could have bought all the equipment necessary and paid for all the calls and still had money to spare!

Finally, note down what new added-value ways of working you could adopt by using IT.

Placing IT at the Centre of Your Communication Strategy

Use the diagram below to consider how IT can help you to be more competitive now, next year and further into the future by putting an effective IT-based communication strategy in place.

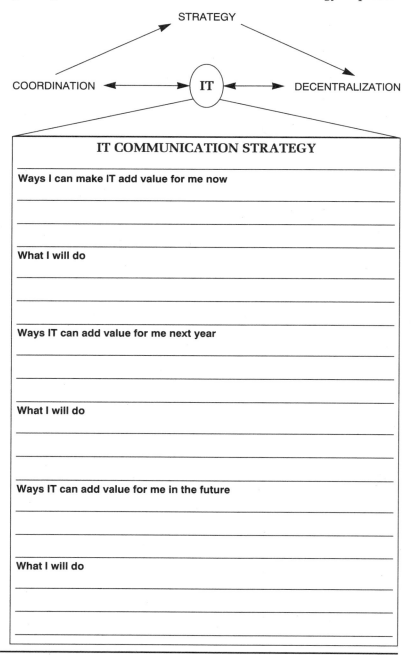

STRATEGY

COORDINATION ◄─────► IT ◄─────► DECENTRALIZATION

IT COMMUNICATION STRATEGY

Ways I can make IT add value for me now

What I will do

Ways IT can add value for me next year

What I will do

Ways IT can add value for me in the future

What I will do

Using IT to Develop Marketspace Opportunities

Use the chart below to explore what marketspace opportunities you can exploit.

First, list three types of information which you use for processes for which you are responsible and which could add value to other operations internal to your organization and then list three which you could share with other organizations to your mutual benefit.

INTERNAL FOCUS		
Information type	Area it would benefit	Benefits (added value) it would provide
EXTERNAL FOCUS		
Information type	Area it would benefit	Benefits (added value) it would provide

Now draw up an action plan to develop the means to share this information for at least one of the three areas you identified.

ACTION PLAN

Revisit this page in six months' time to see what progress you have made. Set up an alarm call in your digital diary to remind you.

IT: The Centre of CompetITiveness

Here are the important points to remember:

- The approach to, and appropriate application of, IT will depend on whether your organization is centralized, integrated, unintegrated or disintegrated.
- Increasingly decentralized organizations cannot benefit from increased responsiveness and flexibility unless excellent communication between the parts is maintained. IT provides a key means to achieve this.
- Effective use of IT to manage information and communication gives you more time to manage people and your job effectively.
- IT enables you to develop new ways of working cooperatively with other organizations and of creating new products and the marketspaces to exploit them.

ACTION POINTS

Use the table overleaf to draw up a summary action plan of how you will apply IT in your organization to increase competitiveness.

MANAGING INFORMATION: ACTION PLAN NO. 4
IT FOR COMPETITIVENESS

IT can help me manage people more effectively by . . .	
IT can help me manage time more effectively by . . .	
IT can help me create marketspace opportunities by . . .	

UNIT 7 Serendipity: What Chance Success?

In this unit you will:

- define the level of serendipity you need for your job
- develop your networks to manage the serendipity you require
- consider how to obtain more from less.

How Much Serendipity?

In previous units we have looked at the importance of IT in manipulating data in many ways to provide insights into the processes we operate or opportunities to use information in different ways. But the creation, refining and distribution of ideas is a human activity and one central to managers. Your success in this area depends on fostering the right human environment and making enough valuable human connections. In a fast-changing and unpredictable world, this requires a level of serendipity.

What is serendipity? *The faculty of making useful and unexpected discoveries by accident.*

The history of scientific discovery is littered with examples of serendipitous discoveries, the momentous discovery of penicillin by Alexander Fleming being only one of many. But Fleming would not have made his discovery if he had not had a sufficiently open and enquiring mind to recognize the potential in what he saw.

- If there is too much order in what we do we do not see opportunities.
- If there is too little order we become confused and sidetracked.

Regardless of our role, we need to be open to the potential of the unexpected and to leave sufficient leeway in what we do for the unexpected to happen. When it does, we should make the opportunity work for us.

The degree of serendipity that you should engineer for yourself will depend on your role. Ask yourself:

How much innovation do I need to bring to my job?

If your answer is 'A lot', you need to create an environment around you that is rich in sources of information so that you can cross-fertilize ideas with sometimes unexpected and useful results.

If your answer is 'Very little', perhaps you need to think again. If you're a manager you should be open to new ideas and encourage innovative thinking in others.

Management is about positive and continuous change. But serendipity needs to be steered, managed and controlled. Without management it can descend into confusion and chaos. One of your tasks is to define the appropriate level of serendipity and manage it.

Insight: **HARNESSING SERENDIPITY**

The invention of the Post-it note by 3M was not intentional. It was an accidental byproduct of another project. 3M had apparently 'invented' a completely useless product – a glue that would not stay stuck. In most companies this would have been billed as another failure, but 3M is structured and managed to encourage happy accidents and to capitalize on them when they occur. The ubiquitous Post-it is just one result. At 3M serendipity is harnessed as a key resource.

Insight: **NEW LAMPS FOR OLD**

OLD MANAGEMENT STYLE	NEW MANAGEMENT STYLE
Manager takes the discoveries of the team and presents them as if he/she was the originator	*Manager gets the originators to do the presentation*
Strives to control and constrain – discourages any challenges	*Strives to liberate – encourages challenges and innovates*
Old teams would follow the party line and have the word handed down	*The new teams range widely and consider all points of view, challenging and seeking to change*

YOU MAY NOW CONTINUE WITH THE NEXT FAST TRACK SECTION ON PAGE 151 OR MOVE TO THE SKILLBUILDER EXERCISE ON PAGES 153–154

Get Connected

Serendipity needs to be **orchestrated and steered** if it is to be useful. One of the most important ways to manage it is through the connections you make. Serendipity depends on making connections; useful serendipity depends on making the **right** connections.

Business is a contact sport – not a contract sport – you need connections!

You can manage your own level of serendipity through establishing, developing and maintaining your own networks both inside and beyond your organization. In establishing your own networks, you should ask:

- Who are the right people to know and talk to?
- What do they do?
- What can I learn from them?
- What can I give to them?
- How can I emulate the best – learning from everyone and everything?

Remember:

- You have to be prepared to give as good as you get. Your networks will wither away if people feel you are unwilling or have nothing to contribute to them.
- Being part of one network gives you access to many others. Be aware and willing to make use of secondary connections. For example, contributing on the Internet to newsgroups relevant to your interests means that you can stretch your network around the world and talk to people you never knew existed, learning from them and sharing ideas. The Internet has catapulted the whole concept of networking into a new dimension.

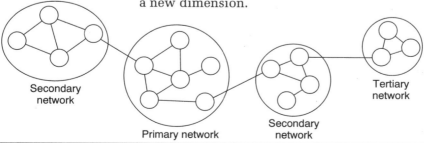

Secondary network

Primary network

Secondary network

Tertiary network

YOU MAY NOW CONTINUE WITH THE NEXT FAST TRACK SECTION ON PAGE 152 OR MOVE TO THE SKILLBUILDER EXERCISE ON PAGES 155–156

Getting More from Less

A significant obstacle to serendipity today is the danger of being overwhelmed by the sheer volume of potentially useful information. Managing the volume of information is a key to success.

***I*nsight:** **THE NAME OF THE ROSE, UMBERTO ECO VERSUS THE INTERNET**

Virtually free access to information is a recent phenomenon. In the past, information and knowledge were closely guarded and access denied to all but the most privileged. In Umberto Eco's famous novel the true content of the library is a closely guarded secret worth committing murder to preserve. Serendipity was virtually non-existent. The librarian existed to impose order and inaccessibility.

Contrast this to the Internet – a super-abundance of information and data with freedom to roam where one will. The potential here for serendipity is enormous. The catch is there is no order – no signposts – and you are far more likely to find what you don't want than what you do, and take some time doing so.

Information is no longer power. Don't hold on to it, communicate it – it's the lubricant of success and needs a low viscosity!

We don't want to go back to the medieval style of controlling information but we do need to evolve modern ways of compressing and organizing information so that we can cope with it.

Think of it as a simple equation:

LESS = MORE

where the information has clarity, brevity and timeliness.

YOU MAY NOW CONTINUE WITH THE NEXT FAST TRACK SECTION ON PAGE 167 OR MOVE TO THE SKILLBUILDER EXERCISE ON PAGES 157–158

How Much Serendipity?

Use the following series of statements to assess the extent to which you encourage serendipity.

Consider each statement and rate it according to the degree with which you believe it applies to you.

STATEMENT	Agree/disagree
1. It is more important to get on and do something than talk about it.	1 2 3 4 5
2. If a thing's worth doing it's worth doing badly (G.K. Chesterton).	1 2 3 4 5
3. I make a point of reading outside my normal field of interests.	1 2 3 4 5
4. I make a point of visiting unusual places.	1 2 3 4 5
5. When hiring people I intentionally look for the out-of-the-ordinary.	1 2 3 4 5
6. I'm not afraid of asking the dumb question.	1 2 3 4 5
7. I encourage people to try out new ideas.	1 2 3 4 5
8. I actively empower people to extend their knowledge and skills through training, coaching, etc.	1 2 3 4 5
9. I applaud failures.	1 2 3 4 5
10. I fight against the 'not invented here' syndrome.	1 2 3 4 5
11. I like to shake things up so people don't get into a rut.	1 2 3 4 5
12. I'm prepared to take time to listen to **anyone**.	1 2 3 4 5
13. I'm not afraid to ignore what others say.	1 2 3 4 5
14. I rely on my intuition rather than rational plans.	1 2 3 4 5
15. I work to break down functional barriers.	1 2 3 4 5
16. I work to break down hierarchies.	1 2 3 4 5
17. I give people access to all information.	1 2 3 4 5
18. I take sabbaticals and encourage others to do so.	1 2 3 4 5
19. I spend time with people outside my organization, including suppliers and customers.	1 2 3 4 5
20. I break up my own personal rhythms and routines.	1 2 3 4 5
21. I see part of my role as a disorganizer.	1 2 3 4 5
22. I see part of my role as a provoker and challenger.	1 2 3 4 5
23. I spend so little time at my desk or office I hardly know where it is.	1 2 3 4 5
24. I try to spend at least one day a week at home.	1 2 3 4 5
25. I try not to interfere but allow people to make mistakes and learn from them.	1 2 3 4 5
26. I take off my jacket, roll up my sleeves and get stuck in.	1 2 3 4 5
27. I encourage enthusiastic commitment among people.	1 2 3 4 5
28. I encourage renegades.	1 2 3 4 5

SKILLBUILDER

Add up your total score for all the statements.

- If you scored 56 or less, you tend to encourage a serendipitous environment.
- If you scored 57 to 111, you allow some fluidity but like to keep a fair degree of control and order.
- If you scored 112 or more, you discourage serendipity and prefer a world of order and predictability.

It is not a question of one approach being better than another. It depends on your organization and your role. In a fast-changing world, however, you should ask yourself whether you can keep pace with, and possibly contribute to, changes around you if you prefer a very rigidly controlled environment.

The importance of serendipity is underlined by the development of data mining software to search out interesting, but unexpected, connections between pieces of data.

Get Connected

Use your answers to the following questions to help identify who makes up your primary network. This may well include people outside your organization.

1. The people I enjoy chatting to most are:

_____

_____

2. The people I rely on most to help me in my job are:

_____

_____

3. I can gain useful information from:

_____

_____

4. The people I approach for good ideas are:

_____

_____

5. People who frequently come to me for information, ideas or advice are:

_____

_____

For the people you have identified in your network, complete the table below. If there are people you want to add to your network, use the table to assess what they can offer you and vice versa.

Person's name	What they offer me now	What they could offer in future	What I offer them now	What I can offer them in future

Now make a list of actions that will help you to build and strengthen your network. We give some examples to get you started.

Type of action	Comments
Visit a department I know little about	
Ask a colleague for advice	
Do people favours where I can	
Ask dumb questions	
Probe – seek to understand	
Suggest alternatives	
Be catalytic in bringing others together	
Identify useful Internet newsgroups and develop new connections	

SKILLBUILDER

Getting More from Less

Develop strategies for compressing and organizing information into manageable proportions.

Remember, from Unit 2, the three categories of information:

- useless
- distracting
- useful.

Discard the *useless* information immediately.

For the *useful* information adopt compression techniques. For example:

- find digests and abstracts that already compress the information for you
- create your own digests and abstracts – make notes and reminders
- develop diagrammatic representations of the ideas (for example, Mind Maps®) that you can use instead of the original. Remember, a picture is worth 1000 words.

Adopt ways of organizing information for quick access and easy reference. For example:

- a quick-reference card system
- a database on your PC with cross-references
- Insert your own bookmarks and such like on the Internet to find your way to where you want to go quickly.

For the *distracting* information develop your own category system as a holding pen in which to store the information until it can be treated as useful. Constantly review the material in your holding pen and discard anything you haven't used after six months, unless there is a very specific task for which you are keeping it. The criterion for storing information should not be that it *might* be useful but that it *will be* useful.

In addition, put time aside to do the following.

- Use a search engine to regularly scan your general interest topic areas on the Internet.

- Network with others to increase your chances of picking up new information.
- Initiate lively discussions and debates during coffee, lunch and tea breaks – develop your own information cafe.
- Encourage and educate people, by regular communication, to send you relevant and useful ideas, news and views – and reciprocate!

Serendipity: What Chance Success?

Here are the important points to remember.

- You need to manage the generation of chance opportunities for innovation according to the type of role you occupy.
- The networks you create are crucial in managing the creation of beneficial chance opportunities.
- Too much information can stifle creativity.

ACTION POINTS

Map out your exposure to interesting new ideas that could transform your work. Change and/or add to the list below:

Newspapers I read	
Journals/magazines I read	
Professional bodies to which I contribute	
Hobbies I pursue	

Sports I play	
Friends with whom I share ideas	
TV programmes I watch	
Internet newsgroups to which I contribute	
Internet sites I visit	
Holidays/trips I take	
My heroes!	

PART

III

How to Use IT to Manage Effectively

At the end of **Part III** you will be able to:

- design your own style of management that harnesses the benefits of IT to meet both your needs and those with whom you work
- help others to manage information more effectively.

Introduction: Developing the Right Mindset

Decentralization, if it is matched by effective communication, should not mean a loss of control or influence. It should mean working smarter by liberating people to work in ways that are best for them and the organization. People should feel that they are empowered, part of a team and net contributors to the enterprise, not that they are insignificant cogs in a huge machine.

If you trust people to behave responsibly – and the vast majority will – you give yourself the opportunity to use the advantages of IT to give individuals the freedom to fulfil their potential while still retaining control and providing the guidance necessary to meet your managerial objectives. However, you must be tolerant of errors and people carrying out tasks in unusual and unexpected ways.

Advances in IT mean that you and your teams don't need to be tied to your desks. You can work from home, at other remote locations or 'on the road' with, for example, customers and suppliers. As a manager, you have to find the most effective ways of managing this much more fluid situation.

IT cannot turn a bad manager into a good one – it is no substitute for poor or underdeveloped management skills. However, in the hands of a competent manager, IT provides the means to manage more flexibly in the increasingly fluid business environment.

Insight: **WHO HAS THE ANSWERS?**

In today's increasingly fast-moving world you cannot afford to believe that you, alone, have all the answers. Consider some of the statements from some famous people from the more certain past. If they could be so wrong, why shouldn't you be?

'I think there is a world market for maybe five computers.' (Thomas Watson, chairman of IBM, 1943)

'I have travelled the length and breadth of this country and talked with the best people, and I can assure you that data processing is a fad that won't last out the year.' (The editor in charge of business books for Prentice Hall, 1957)

'There is no reason anyone would want a computer in their home.' (Ken Olson, president, chairman and founder of Digital Equipment Corporation, 1977)

'This "telephone" has too many shortcomings to be seriously considered as a means of communication. The device is inherently of no value to us.' (Western Union internal memo, 1876)

'Who the hell wants to hear actors talk?' (H.M. Warner, Warner Brothers, 1927)

'We don't like their sound, and guitar music is on the way out.' (Decca Recording Co. rejecting the Beatles, 1962)

'Heavier-than-air flying machines are impossible.' (Lord Kelvin, president, Royal Society, 1895)

'Drill for oil? You mean drill into the ground to try and find oil? You're crazy.' (Drillers who Edwin L. Drake tried to enlist into his project to drill for oil in 1859)

'Stocks have reached what looks like a permanently high plateau.' (Irving Fisher, Professor of Economics, Yale University, 1929)

'Airplanes are interesting toys but of no military value.' (Maréchal Ferdinand Foch, Professor of Strategy, Ecole Supérieure de Guerre)

'Everything that can be invented has been invented.' (Charles H. Duell, Commissioner, US Office of Patents, 1899)

'Louis Pasteur's theory of germs is ridiculous fiction.' (Pierre Pachet, Professor of Physiology at Toulouse, 1872)

'640K ought to be enough for anybody.' (Bill Gates, 1981)

The Loneliness of the Long-Distance Manager

In this unit you will:

- consider the attributes and skills required to be a manager in the information age
- explore how IT can help you to manage individuals and teams at a distance.

Asking the Right Questions

To see if you have sufficiently developed the appropriate management skills to use information technology as an effective management tool, use the Skillbuilder on pages 173–74 to gain feedback from those whom you manage.

The information age means an age of continuous learning, not only about the world around us, but also about ourselves and how well we are adapting to cope with the constant change. The best way to learn about ourselves is to ask those around us how they see us.

> Never tell people how to do something. Just tell them what to do and they will amaze you with their ingenuity. (General George Patton)

The questionnaire looks at four important aspects of a manager – your ability to:

- develop and maintain effective work procedures
- foster innovation and creativity
- get the best from people
- provide leadership.

Acting on the Answers

If you have been brave enough to solicit feedback from your team, don't make the most common mistake of all and ignore it!

The feedback you have gained is extremely valuable information. Use it to further your own development and, therefore, that of others. To do this, use the diagram on page 175, develop a profile for yourself that will indicate the strengths on which to build and the areas where you need to develop your skills further. A completed example profile is shown below.

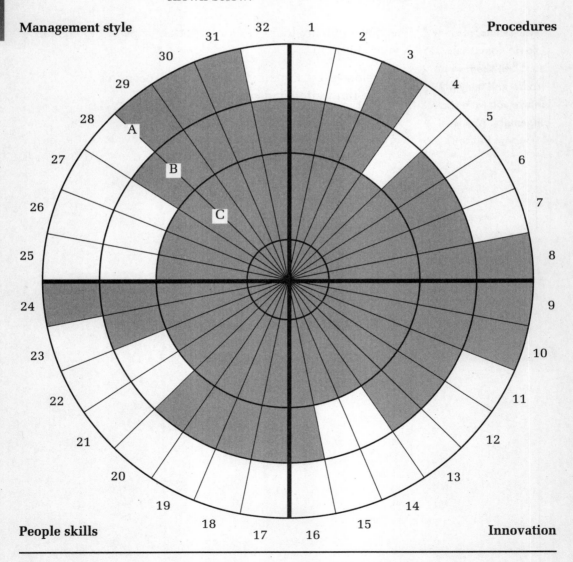

In each of the four areas delineated on the diagram effective information management skills form an important component. These are discussed below.

DEVELOPING EFFECTIVE WORK PROCEDURES

Decentralized and more flexible working patterns require more, rather than less, attention to working procedures. Giving people the freedom to work more effectively is no excuse for abdicating your responsibilities to set a well-developed and clearly understood framework within which people can work effectively. Before you can adopt more flexible working and develop an IT strategy to support it, both you and your team need to have confidence in the work parameters.

FOSTERING INNOVATION AND CREATIVITY

One of the chief benefits of decentralization and increased flexibility is an increase in innovatory ideas for ways of doing the work. However, a supportive and encouraging environment is required for this type of innovation to flourish. Decentralization and a highly judgemental style do not fit together.

GETTING THE BEST FROM PEOPLE

If people are to be encouraged to become more responsible for themselves and to take on more responsibility, they have to be managed consciously for development and growth. A management style that keeps people 'in their place' does not fit with decentralization. Who are you developing to take your place?

PROVIDING LEADERSHIP

Decentralization not only requires more, rather than less, expert management but also management that demonstrates leadership and can foster cooperation and cohesion among decentralized components.

Managing Information to Manage at a Distance

How do you manage information to communicate, stay in control and know what's happening in a dispersed and decentralized organization?

Spending time with people is the most effective way of communicating and managing. We have seen how using IT to manage information effectively creates more time to walk the floor and talk to people, thereby enabling you to:

- communicate, stay in touch and avoid misunderstandings
- be in control
- act **and be effective.**

In the decentralized organization the effective use of IT is even more essential in helping you to maintain control and direction, since it provides you and your team with the means to communicate with each other almost as effectively as if you were meeting face-to-face. Furthermore, it can be used to enable geographically dispersed individuals to work together as a team on the same piece of work – for example, writing a report, designing a product or discussing a work-related issue.

Information technology can eliminate the negative effects of distance through such techniques as:

- use of electronic networking or intranets and extracts
- virtual teamworking
- use of e-mail (floating free) as opposed to the fax (tied down).

With e-mail and electronic networking it is easy – indeed necessary – to adopt a terse and economic style, but take care that it's not misinterpreted as indifference. Similarly, you cannot convey your enthusiasm in a video conference or over the telephone unless you 'overact'! So let people get to know you in real life before you manage remotely.

*I*nsight: CHILDREN AT HEART

Being responsive as a manager is all-important. If you have a child at school and they come home excited by some work or personal achievement, then they need instant attention. Your team are the same – they need a rapid response and a high level of interest. Use IT to reach them and respond to their ideas and questions quickly. Responding with positive questions, challenges and suggestions has the most beneficial effect – you are seen to be interested and taking the trouble to understand.

It would be naive to believe that the freedom information technology brings will always be positive. There will always be a few who will abuse freedom – sometimes, but very rarely, with disastrous consequences. As a manager it's your responsibility to ensure that freedom is matched by accountability. This is covered in more detail in Unit 9.

YOU MAY NOW CONTINUE WITH THE NEXT FAST TRACK SECTION ON PAGE 183 OR MOVE TO THE SKILLBUILDER EXERCISE ON PAGES 177–178

Asking the Right Questions

Distribute the following feedback sheet to all those whom you manage and offer them the opportunity to give you anonymous feedback on your style of management.

PROCEDURES: My manager:		INNOVATION: My manager:	
1. Holds effective team meetings	a. Regularly b. Occasionally c. Never	9. Encourages experimentation	a. Regularly b. Occasionally c. Never
2. Has developed and uses effective systems of communication	a. In all areas b. In some areas c. Not at all	10. Persecutes failure	a. Never b. Occasionally c. Regularly
3. Organizes the work of the team	a. Very effectively b. Fairly effectively c. Ineffectively	11. Takes time to listen to people's ideas	a. Regularly b. Occasionally c. Never
4. Has established means for the self-development of all staff	a. Very effectively b. Fairly effectively c. Ineffectively	12. Will take up a good idea no matter where it came from	a. All the time b. Occasionally c. Never
5. Ensures equal opportunities for all	a. All the time b. Usually – can be biased c. Rarely – is often biased	13. Likes to shake things up	a. Regularly b. Occasionally c. Never
6. Has established regular means of receiving and giving feedback	a. Very effectively b. Fairly effectively c. Ineffectively	14. Stands aside and lets people make mistakes	a. Regularly b. Occasionally c. Never
7. Strives to streamline our admin systems	a. Regularly b. Occasionally c. Never	15. Encourages communication across all frontiers	a. All the time b. Occasionally c. Never
8. Sets clear objectives for the team	a. Very effectively b. Fairly effectively c. Ineffectively	16. Keeps all information to him/herself	a. Never b. Occasionally c. Regularly

SKILLBUILDER

PEOPLE SKILLS: My manager

17. Is fair in dealing with all team members
   a. All the time
   b. Usually
   c. Rarely

18. Conveys to us feelings of:
   a. Security
   b. Indifference
   c. Fear and insecurity

19. Treats all individuals with:
   a. Respect
   b. Indifference
   c. Lack of consideration

20. Motivates me
   a. Highly
   b. To some extent
   c. Not at all

21. Involves me . . .
   a. In all appropriate matters
   b. In most appropriate matters
   c. Not at all

22. In a crisis is . . .
   a. A positive asset
   b. Of little effect
   c. A hindrance

23. Recognizes and rewards positive achievements
   a. Regularly
   b. Occasionally
   c. Never

24. Fosters good working relations between all team members
   a. Very effectively
   b. Fairly effectively
   c. Ineffectively

MANAGEMENT STYLE: My manager

25. Is happy for team members to be better than him/her at work-related tasks
   a. All the time
   b. Occasionally
   c. Never

26. Seeks to develop productive relationships with team members
   a. Very effectively
   b. Fairly effectively
   c. Ineffectively

27. Would rather develop existing individuals than acquire extra staff
   a. All the time
   b. Occasionally
   c. Never

28. Represents the organization . . .
   a. Very well
   b. Competently
   c. Poorly

29. Is . . .
   a. Very trustworthy
   b. Usually trustworthy
   c. Untrustworthy

30. Prefers individuals who can get on with the job without having to refer to him/her
   a. Usually
   b. Occasionally
   c. Never

31. Seeks opportunities to develop individuals
   a. All the time
   b. Occasionally
   c. Never

32. Is relaxed, friendly and approachable
   a. All the time
   b. Occasionally
   c. Never

A further interesting exercise is to count the number of times you respond positively and negatively to the people around you. In this new mode of tolerance and empowerment you will struggle to satisfy the needs of your organization and your people whilst coping with new and established pressures. No matter how tough the going becomes, you must remain upbeat, encouraging and positive. Use a chart to monitor your positive and negative responses. If you score less than 70 per cent positive you have problems!

Acting on the Answers

Use the answers to the feedback questionnaire on pages 173–74 to construct a profile of your strengths and weaknesses in diagrammatic form. In the profile chart below each segment is numbered to correspond to a question on the feedback questionnaire.

For each question work out, from all the responses which have been returned, whether you have an A, B or C score based on the percentage of As, Bs or Cs you received. If you have an 'A' score for a question, mark along the outer line of the segment. Mark 'B' scores along the middle line and 'C' scores on the inner line. The example profile on page 168 shows how this works:

- Shade up to the inner line to indicate areas you need to develop.
- Shade up to the middle line to indicate areas of competence.
- Shade up to the outer line to indicate areas of strength to build upon.

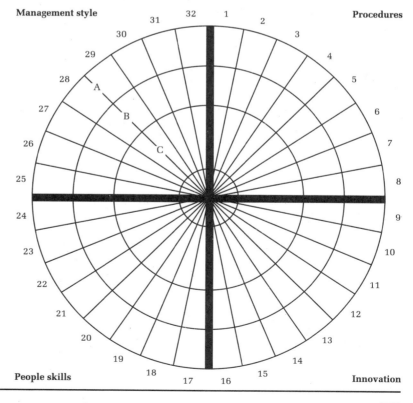

When you have completed the profile, devise an action plan to develop those areas where feedback has indicated that you could improve.

MANAGING INFORMATION: ACTION PLAN NO. 5	
I can improve my management style by . . .	
I can improve procedures by . . .	
I can develop my people skills by . . .	
I can develop a more innovative environment by . . .	

Managing Information to Manage at a Distance

Use the exercise below to find out what is required to link up your staff and make them capable of operating as a team over a distance. Consider what you will need to achieve the synthesis of dispersion and cooperation in the short, medium and long term – in other words:

- what you can do now, with what you've got
- what you can do in a year's time
- what may take a little longer.

Current team functions	Future team functions	Short-term information management solutions	Medium-term information management solutions	Long-term information management solutions
1.				
2.				
3.				
4.				
5.				

SKILLBUILDER

MAKE YOUR TEAM A MULTIMEDIA TEAM

As part of your normal management style, you need to encourage people to use all the media.

- Ask for more details – pictures, diagrams, business cases – whilst you are on the move.
- Use electronic working to keep briefed and up-to-date.
- Post programme reports on a noticeboard for all to access and see. The central vision and overall scheme of operation can be displayed in a single space along with barometer displays of expenditure, timescales met and deliverables.
- Make it easy for everyone to understand where they fit in, what their contribution is, and how the team/company is doing. Electronic working can do this instantly and with relative ease.

Remember that technology is your servant – and not the other way around. Using technology for technology's sake is not very smart! Always ask the fundamental question: 'What is right for me, my people, my organization and my customers?' Denying technology is just plain stupid! Using the appropriate technology is smart!

SKILLBUILDER

The Loneliness of the Long-Distance Manager

Here are the important points to remember:

- IT cannot turn a bad manager into a good one, but it can help good ones to manage more flexibly in the increasingly fluid business environment.
- Using IT effectively helps to overcome the negative impact of distance, enabling you and each member of your team to keep in touch with each other and work cooperatively wherever they are.

ACTION POINTS

1. Use the questionnaire on your management style on pages 173–74 to obtain feedback from your team and/or colleagues on your management style.
2. Based on the results, draw up a development plan to improve your skills in appropriate areas.
3. In six months' time, ask the same people to answer the questionnaire again. Check the results to see if you have improved and draw up another development plan.
4. Get your colleagues to do the same and share the resulting insights.

Managing Information: Redefining Your Role

In this unit you will develop a programme to:

- **control your information flows**
- **make your team information managers**
- **develop an empowered team**
- **encourage innovation for competitiveness**
- **maintain effective feedback**
- **develop your replacement**
- **become a centre of excellence.**

Introduction

Management is about change – positive and beneficial change. Your job is to invoke change in a creative way but always with a purpose – not just for the sake of it!

To work smarter you have continually to redefine and develop your role. In this unit you have the opportunity to develop your own seven-step action plan to help you become a manager of information in the information age.

As was emphasized in Unit 2, good information management depends on achieving:

- efficiency
- effectiveness
- empowerment.

The template on page 202 gives you a framework to use to help in planning the approaches to take in redefining your role for the information age.

The remainder of this unit provides you with some hints for developing your own action plan.

Step 1: Controlling Your Information Flows

As a manager one of your key tasks is to manage the information flow of that part of your organization for which you are responsible. Information is the fuel that drives the organization forward.

You need to be efficient and effective yourself – only receiving the right information, using it for a purpose and then transmitting it, in a usable form, by the most efficient channel – in other words, **adding value.**

Look back at Unit 4, 'Your Information Audit'. If you have completed your audit you should have the answers to these questions.

1. **Controlling information flows**

   - What information do I need?
   - Why do I need it?
   - How will I use it?
   - From whom/where can I get it?
   - When do I need it?
   - In what form do I need it?
   - What information do others need from me? (This includes asking 'Why?', 'When?' and 'How?' questions.)
   - What unnecessary data am I receiving?
   - What useful and necessary information am I getting too slowly, in the wrong form and so on?
   - What filters can I put in place to deflect or divert information?
   - Who should I communicate it to, in what format and by what means?

Each member of your team could do the same exercise using the Skillbuilder table on page 191.

Remember, you are managing information to:

- increase the efficiency of internal and external processes
- gain competitive advantage in the conventional marketplace
- do more with less and invoke continual change
- drive down costs and increase output
- maintain and extend databases and contacts
- extend your influence and contribution – your added value
- improve the responsiveness of yourself, your staff and your organization
- create new market opportunities and competitive advantage in the evolving marketspace.

YOU MAY NOW CONTINUE WITH THE NEXT FAST TRACK SECTION ON PAGE 185 OR MOVE TO THE SKILLBUILDER EXERCISE ON PAGES 191–192

Step 2: Making Your Team Information Managers

Make sure that your staff and colleagues manage information in the same effective manner as you do yourself. You should also foster a degree of experimentation and creativity. You cannot do it all by yourself or singlehandedly – you need to encourage everyone to contribute and buy in. If your team builds a future together, rather than has the future imposed on it, the benefits will be far greater. It is this that will make your organization competitive.

You can ask members of your team to go through the audit process as summarized in Step 1. But, in order to make this effective, they – like you – need to take on the attributes of an information manager. Encourage them to adopt characteristics of:

- the prospector
- the refiner
- the processor
- the cleanser
- the transporter
- the communicator

as explained in Units 2 and 3.

2. **Making your team information managers**
   Becoming **prospectors** – creating data networks
   Becoming **refiners** – turning data into information
   Becoming efficient **processors** – handling only what is necessary
   Becoming **cleansers** – eliminating waste data
   Becoming efficient **transporters** – matching the message to the medium
   Becoming effective **communicators** – keeping communications brief and simple.

YOU MAY NOW CONTINUE WITH THE NEXT FAST TRACK SECTION ON PAGE 186 OR MOVE TO THE SKILLBUILDER EXERCISE ON PAGE 193

Step 3: Developing Responsibility and Accountability

Spreading information – especially high-quality information – involves spreading power. This brings about the death of hierarchy and – with electronic working – the death of geography! But this does not mean that chaos will prevail. With power comes responsibility. Once everyone has access to information, everyone becomes responsible and accountable.

If, as it should be, part of your information management strategy is to divert or spread the flow of information throughout your team, this must be for a purpose. You will remember from Unit 1 that information only has meaning once it has purpose.

Do not expect to achieve results by merely releasing information; you must plan for its use and draw up clear guidelines.

3. **Developing responsibility and accountability**
   As you make more information available to your team, you need to establish clearly:

   - what information you are providing
   - what power this gives the individual
   - how you expect that power to be used
   - what limits you want to place on that power – that is, the limits of both your and others' responsibilities – setting clear and well-understood boundaries
   - how you will make the individual accountable for the use of that power
   - how you will recognize and reward the appropriate and profitable use of that power.

YOU MAY NOW CONTINUE WITH THE NEXT FAST TRACK SECTION ON PAGE 187 OR MOVE TO THE SKILLBUILDER EXERCISE ON PAGE 194

Step 4: Encouraging Innovation to Stay Competitive

We have seen how IT can be the centre of your competitive strategy. But IT not only creates change, it constantly changes itself allowing the development of new working patterns and configurations. This process requires you to be flexible and constantly prepared to adopt new ways of working. It also requires you to encourage your team to be flexible and innovative as well.

An environment that encourages innovation has to be created and nurtured – it does not necessarily happen on its own. You need to cultivate the right level of serendipity (Unit 7) and adopt an encouraging management style (Unit 8).

4. **Encouraging innovation to stay competitive**
   What can I do to:

   - enable individuals to try out new ideas?
   - extend the skills and knowledge of team members?
   - encourage cross-fertilization of ideas between departments?
   - enable individuals to make mistakes in safety?
   - make sure that people learn from their mistakes?
   - develop productive working relationships between all team members?
   - recognize and reward positive achievements?

YOU MAY NOW CONTINUE WITH THE NEXT FAST TRACK SECTION ON PAGE 188
OR MOVE TO THE SKILLBUILDER EXERCISE ON PAGE 195

Step 5: Maintaining Effective Feedback

The spread of information and the resulting decline of hierarchies makes it vital that you recognize that you work as part of a team. This means that to manage effectively, you require information about yourself from bottom-up and peer group reviews.

> 20/20 vision is having a 360-degree view of your performance.

5. **Bottom-up and peer review**
   Obtain regular and objective feedback on my performance from my team and colleagues in terms of my:

   - handling of procedures
   - handling of people
   - encouragement of innovation
   - personal style in fostering effective working relationships.

YOU MAY NOW CONTINUE WITH THE NEXT FAST TRACK SECTION ON PAGE 189
OR MOVE TO THE SKILLBUILDER EXERCISE ON PAGE 196

Step 6: Developing Your Replacement

One of your roles is to be a constructive agent for change. An essential part of that role is to develop individuals who are capable of replacing you.

If you are indispensable:

- how can you move on?
- how can the organization benefit from new ideas that are beyond the limits of your imagination?

Insight: **DON'T HANG AROUND TOO LONG**

Those that start revolutions usually hang around too long, creating new rigidities that eventually stifle new initiatives. The people needed to start a new business are seldom the people you would wish to run it once it is successful!

Make it one of your top priorities to develop your replacement. You can use a coaching framework to achieve this. In discussion with your team members you can agree on appropriate areas for development for which coaching assignments would form an appropriate solution.

6. Developing your replacement

Put in place a coaching programme to develop the relevant skills:

- What are the areas for development?
- What are the objectives?
- What is the current situation?
- What are the options for development?
- What are the action steps?
- What is the extent of authority?
- What has been agreed?

Insight: **SOLUTIONS NOT PROBLEMS**

As a general principle, never go to your boss with problems – only solutions!

YOU MAY NOW CONTINUE WITH THE NEXT FAST TRACK SECTION ON PAGE 190 OR MOVE TO THE SKILLBUILDER EXERCISE ON PAGES 197–198

189

Step 7: Being a Centre of Excellence

As an agent for change you must lead by example. The effective management of information has to start somewhere and that should be with you. To do this, you need to become your own centre of excellence and spread best practice first in your own team and then through the rest of the organization.

During the process you need to be aware of the fundamental shift in approach that managers have to make in the information age. The power that you hold through access to unlimited information means that you no longer have always to **react** to events, but you can begin to anticipate them and become **proactive**. This may be one of the most significant ways you can add value and secure your future.

The watchwords for the manager in the information age should be:

Thinking
Planning
Anticipating

7. **Being an example to others**
   Take the following steps to become an effective information manager:

   - Become efficient and effective at processing information using IT as a tool of data manipulation.
   - Empower and develop others to manage information efficiently and effectively through the use of IT.
   - Develop skills as a manager of information to create added value in both the marketplace and the marketspace.
   - Make sure that current working methods are sensitive and responsive to changes in information management and IT.

YOU MAY NOW CONTINUE WITH THE MAINTAINING YOUR SKILL SECTION ON PAGE 207 OR MOVE TO THE SKILLBUILDER EXERCISE ON PAGE 199

Step 1: Controlling Your Information Flows

Use copies of the tables below to summarize your information audit.

Item of information I need:	
I need it because . . .	
I will use it to . . .	
I can get it from . . .	
I need it by . . .	
I need it in the form of . . .	
I have problems in . . .	
Steps to resolve this are . . .	

SKILLBUILDER

Item of information needed FROM me:	
It is needed by . . .	
They need it because . . .	
They will use it to . . .	
They need it by . . .	
They need it in the form of . . .	
They have problems in . . .	
Steps to resolve this are . . .	

Step 2: Making Your Team Information Managers

Use the following table to plan out how to develop each team member, or the team as a whole, into information managers.

Role	Do more of	Do less of	Do the same
The prospector			
The refiner			
The processor			
The cleanser			
The transporter			
The communicator			

SKILLBUILDER

Step 3: Developing Responsibility and Accountability

Use the following chart to map out the extent of responsibilities and accountability associated with the release of the power of information.

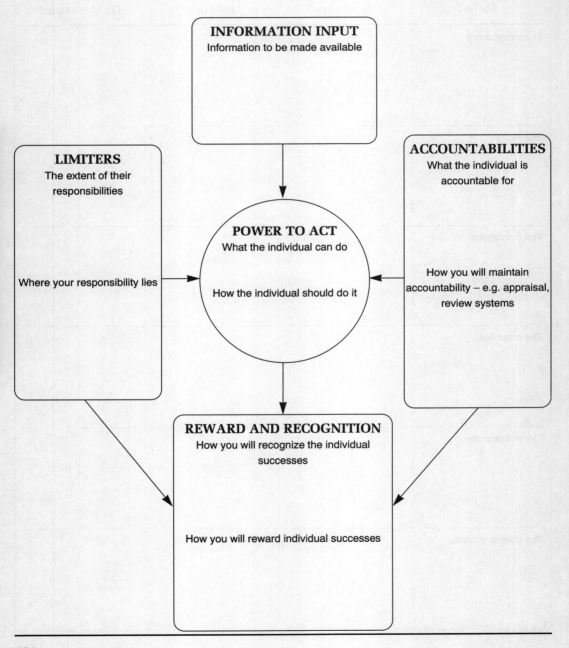

INFORMATION INPUT
Information to be made available

LIMITERS
The extent of their responsibilities

Where your responsibility lies

POWER TO ACT
What the individual can do

How the individual should do it

ACCOUNTABILITIES
What the individual is accountable for

How you will maintain accountability – e.g. appraisal, review systems

REWARD AND RECOGNITION
How you will recognize the individual successes

How you will reward individual successes

Step 4: Encouraging Innovation to Stay Competitive

Use the following chart to map out how you can create a favourable environment for innovation.

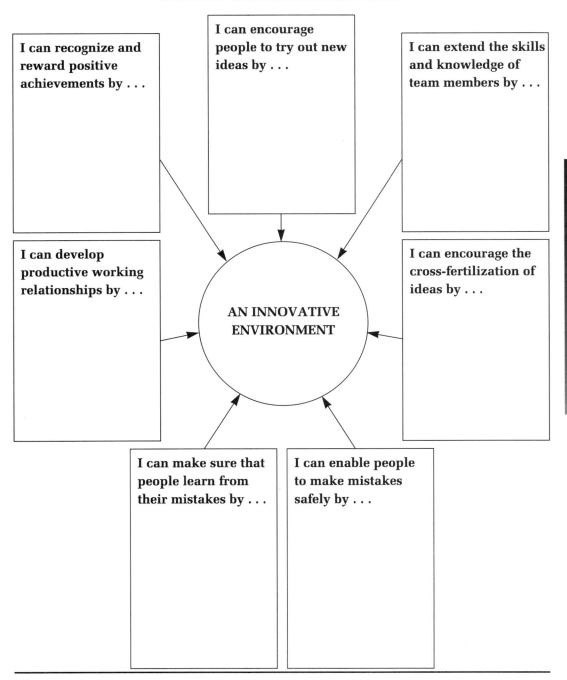

I can recognize and reward positive achievements by . . .

I can encourage people to try out new ideas by . . .

I can extend the skills and knowledge of team members by . . .

I can develop productive working relationships by . . .

I can encourage the cross-fertilization of ideas by . . .

AN INNOVATIVE ENVIRONMENT

I can make sure that people learn from their mistakes by . . .

I can enable people to make mistakes safely by . . .

Step 5: Maintaining Effective Feedback

Use the appraisal questionnaire provided in Unit 8, or one of your own design, to obtain the feedback you need. Repeat this exercise regularly – at least every six months. Assess the results and use the chart below to create your own development plan.

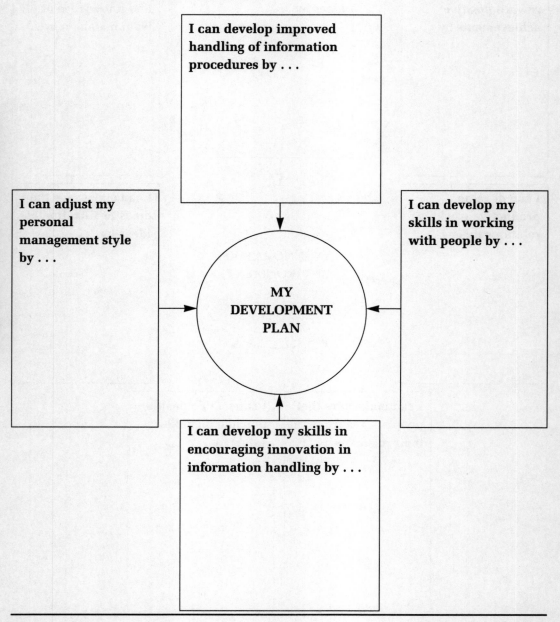

I can develop improved handling of information procedures by . . .

I can adjust my personal management style by . . .

I can develop my skills in working with people by . . .

MY DEVELOPMENT PLAN

I can develop my skills in encouraging innovation in information handling by . . .

Step 6: Developing Your Replacement

Use the following framework to plan coaching assignments for your team members with the objective of developing them into your replacement. Developing any such plan must be a joint effort – jointly agreed and committed to.

1. Agree the assignment	What are the reasons? What is the relevance?
2. Identify the objectives	What is the desired outcome? What specific, measurable objectives can be defined?
3. Explore the current situation	What is the current level of skill/knowledge? What are the current difficulties? What is important?

4. **Explore options**	What are the options?
	What are the priorities?
	What resources may be needed?
5. Develop the action plan	What needs to be done?
	When is it to be done by?
	What are the likely problems?
6. Give freedom to act	What support is needed?
	What authority is needed to complete the assignment?
7. What has been agreed?	What have we agreed?
	What are the agreed next steps?

Step 7: Being a Centre of Excellence

Use the table below to start planning how to become a centre of excellence.

ACTION	MUST DO NOW	SHOULD DO SOON	COULD DO LATER
Become efficient and effective at processing information using IT as a tool of data manipulation			
Empower and develop others to manage information efficiently and effectively through the use of IT			
Develop skills as a manager of information to create added value in the marketplace and the marketspace			
Make sure that current working methods are sensitive and responsive to changes in information management and IT			

Managing Information: Redefining Your Role

Remember, the seven key points are as follows:

- Manage information efficiently, adding value, so that you have the time to do the real work – that is, manage people.
- Make sure that others work in the same way so that they have time to communicate effectively.
- Recognize that managing people requires information about yourself by maintaining effective feedback.
- Be flexible and prepared constantly to adopt new ways of working that fit more appropriately into the changing environment.
- Lead by example – the effective management of information has to start somewhere. You need to become your own centre of excellence and spread best practice first in your own team and then through the rest of the organization.
- Create the leaders to take your place – those that start revolutions usually hang around too long creating new rigidities. Make it one of your top priorities to develop your replacement.
- Make sure that responsibility and accountability are defined with access to information and the power to use it.

ACTION POINTS

Use the framework overleaf to help you develop your action plan for managing in the information age.

CHECK POINTS

MANAGING INFORMATION FOR EFFICIENCY

1. Controlling my own information flows	2. Making my team information managers

MANAGING PEOPLE FOR EMPOWERMENT

3. Developing responsibility and accountability	4. Encouraging innovation to stay competitive	5. Maintaining effective feedback

MANAGING MYSELF FOR EFFECTIVENESS

6. Developing my replacement	7. Being a centre of excellence

Looking Forward: Where IT Can Take You in the (Not Too Distant) Future

For millennia people have grouped together in small tribes to form effective teams able to survive in various environments. In a team the sum of the component parts is greater than the whole – each member brings something unique to the group and complements the others' skills and experience. In the past the limitations of information storage and communication have always dictated the nature of these tribes – legions, villages, towns, cities, companies and organizations.

Information technology brings the opportunity to create new organizations which are largely independent of location. We no longer have to be within shouting or walking distance of other people. Telecommunications has shrunk the world, and computers have made it intelligent and accessible. So, in some respects, we are now witnessing the demise of geography, but still suffer the constraints of time zones and the international date line. What will happen next? What conditions are you likely to encounter over the next 20 years? Consider the following facts:

- Twenty-five years ago the average graduate expected to work for only three organizations during a 40-year working life. Today that number has grown to 7 and in the next 10 years it will exceed 15.
- A university degree used to be an education for life, and a vocation was a permanent objective. Today a monotonic career is rare and many degrees have a half-life of only seven years. This makes a series of higher degrees a necessity. Education is becoming a continuum.
- Companies are changing their structure from that of a large permanent employee base and a few contractors to that of an essential few permanent employees and a large contractor contingent.
- Individuals are moving away from working for a single employer serially towards working for multiple employers in parallel.

- Companies used to be vertically integrated with the capability to carry out total projects on a few sites. More and more will become virtualized as they concentrate on project management and coordination and contract out significant portions of their activity.
- Whereas companies used to compete head-to-head in the marketplace, they now have to collaborate, even if they are in a state of litigation over some activities.
- Leading companies now bring product to market in less than nine months by simultaneously working round the clock and round the world. As operations come to the end of the day in the UK, then they are passed on to the West Coast of the USA, and then to the Pacific Rim to start the cycle again. This cannot be achieved without IT and people skilled in its use. Without this capability many businesses would no longer be global and would not be able to compete or survive.
- Business organizations will increasingly take the form of multicellular organisms of people and small companies. They will come together to achieve an objective, complete the programme, and then disband.

All the above developments demand:

- people with good IT skills
- creative and innovative people who can use electronic working to shrink distance and time and become ultra-productive.

As a manager you can opt out, but you can't escape!

Remember:

- Common sense is an increasingly rare commodity!
- Technology should be used appropriately to gain advantage – not because it is fashionable or because someone says so!
- You cannot lead from the back!
- You cannot do it all yourself!

Look out for:

- managers who install a secretary between themselves and the keyboard
- those who print out pages from the screen
- those who resist technology and change
- the ineffective and ineffectual

and try to help them see the light!

Identifying Areas for Further Development

Now that you have completed this Workbook use the questionnaire, taken from the Introduction and reproduced below, to assess your level of skill in managing information and to identify areas in which you would like to develop further.

Assess your skill level by circling the appropriate number in each case.

Skill area	Skill level					Unit	Importance of development area				
	High				Low		High				Low
	1	2	3	4	5		1	2	3	4	5
Identifying the difference between useful information and distracting or irrelevant data	1	2	3	4	5	1	1	2	3	4	5
Applying the four principles of information management	1	2	3	4	5	1	1	2	3	4	5
Accessing, refining and processing information to achieve goals	1	2	3	4	5	2	1	2	3	4	5
Discarding, transmitting and communicating information effectively	1	2	3	4	5	3	1	2	3	4	5
Auditing the value of information required to do a job or task	1	2	3	4	5	4	1	2	3	4	5
Managing the in- and outflow of information needed to perform effectively	1	2	3	4	5	5	1	2	3	4	5
Minimizing paperwork and organizing information flow and retrieval	1	2	3	4	5	5	1	2	3	4	5

Skill area	Skill level					Unit	Importance of development area				
	High				**Low**		**High**				**Low**
	1	**2**	**3**	**4**	**5**		**1**	**2**	**3**	**4**	**5**
Coordinating activities in a decentralizing organization	1	2	3	4	5	6	1	2	3	4	5
Using information technology to enhance competitiveness by creating more time for people and reducing travelling time	1	2	3	4	5	6	1	2	3	4	5
Harnessing information technology to manage inventiveness and creativity	1	2	3	4	5	7	1	2	3	4	5
Managing and developing people effectively at a distance with the aid of IT	1	2	3	4	5	8	1	2	3	4	5
Implementing a coherent plan to manage information and to become a manager in the information age	1	2	3	4	5	9	1	2	3	4	5

PREPARING A DEVELOPMENT PLAN

Use the table below to define your development plan for those areas you have identified as important.

Skill area	What I want to develop	How I can develop
Identifying the difference between useful information and distracting or irrelevant data		
Applying the four principles of information management		
Accessing, refining and processing information to achieve goals		

Skill area	What I want to develop	How I can develop
Discarding, transmitting and communicating information effectively		
Auditing the value of information required to do a job or task		
Managing the in- and outflow of information needed to perform effectively		
Minimizing paperwork and organizing information flow and retrieval		
Coordinating activities in a decentralizing organization		
Using information technology to enhance competitiveness by creating more time for people and reducing travelling time		
Harnessing information technology to manage inventiveness and creativity		
Managing and developing people effectively at a distance with the aid of IT		
Implementing a coherent plan to manage information and to become a manager in the information age		

Your Support Network

If you are going to become an effective change agent, you will need support to keep you motivated and confident and as a means of obtaining meaningful feedback. Use the table below to help you develop your own support network.

Type of support	At my job	Away from my job
Someone I can learn from		
Someone with whom I can discuss the self-help exercises I have completed		
Someone who helps me focus on my strengths		
Someone who gives me constructive feedback		
Someone who is always a valuable source of information		
Someone who will challenge me to take a good look at myself		
Someone with whom I can share my disappointments		
Someone who introduces me to new ideas, new interests, new people		
Someone I can confide in		

Extending Your Knowledge

One problem with information management and IT is that the pace of change is so rapid that anything that is presented on the topic is almost immediately out-of-date – including this book! So your problem lies not only in extending your knowledge but also in trying to keep up with new developments. The following mind map may give you a few ideas.

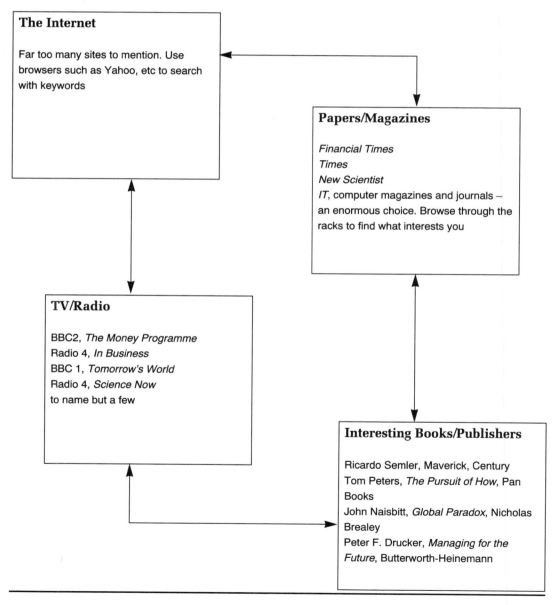

The Internet

Far too many sites to mention. Use browsers such as Yahoo, etc to search with keywords

Papers/Magazines

Financial Times
Times
New Scientist
IT, computer magazines and journals – an enormous choice. Browse through the racks to find what interests you

TV/Radio

BBC2, *The Money Programme*
Radio 4, *In Business*
BBC 1, *Tomorrow's World*
Radio 4, *Science Now*
to name but a few

Interesting Books/Publishers

Ricardo Semler, Maverick, Century
Tom Peters, *The Pursuit of How*, Pan Books
John Naisbitt, *Global Paradox*, Nicholas Brealey
Peter F. Drucker, *Managing for the Future*, Butterworth-Heinemann